The Culture of Crime

The Culture of Crime

Edited by
Craig L. LaMay
and
Everette E. Dennis

TRANSACTION PUBLISHERS
New Brunswick (U.S.A.) and London (U.K.)

Library of Congress Catalog Number: 95-7674
ISBN: 1-56000-826-1
Printed in the United States of America

Library of Congress Cataloging-in-Publication Data

The culture of crime / edited by Craig L. LaMay and Everette E. Dennis.
    p. cm.
Includes bibliographical references and index.
ISBN 1-56000-826-1 (alk. paper)
    1. Crime in mass media—United States.   2. Mass media—Social aspects—United States.   3. Mass media—United States—Psychological aspects. I. LaMay, Craig L. II. Dennis, Everette E.
P96.C74C85 1995
364.1'0973—dc20   95-7674
                                     CIP

Contents

Part I Overview

Crime news helped catapult the penny press to dizzying new levels of circulation in 19th-century urban America, but nothing quite matched the *National Police Gazette*—a 16-page journal of sex, race baiting, sports and violence, replete with lurid illustrations and printed on pink paper. Scorned by the elite press, says the author, an American studies scholar, the *Gazette* and its publisher, Richard Kyle Fox, now seem visionary, having set the tone—for better or worse—for the tabloids and television of today.

Certainly the news media's obsession with violent crime creates a public image at odds with statistical data on crime, says a Hunter College sociologist, but he asks of the reader what one editor asked of him: "How would *you* cover it?" The author answers by arguing for a better and more informed sensationalism: "Be explicit, pull no punches, leave no doubts, forget the euphemisms. Don't make the story palatable. The real story usually isn't, and readers should know that."

"Behold the entrails of any large American newspaper's metro section"— "misdemeanor homicides" that will be interred as filler on page D17. The author, police reporter for the *Baltimore Sun*, argues that this is the very essence of what journalism should not be: "writing and reporting that anesthetizes readers, that cleans and simplifies the violence and cruelty of a dirty, complex world," and he returns the reader to the "lost legacy of American crime reporting, a grand and noble tradition of ambulance chasing that has been squandered in the modern crusade for our feigned, practiced objectivity."

Part II Views on Crime and Media

"I heard the crowd cry out, 'It's the MOTHER! That's Jennifer's MOTHER!!' and suddenly I was swallowed up in a near riot, the police pushing reporters, reporters yelling questions at me, cameramen snapping pictures. I turned in disbelief and screamed, 'My God, what's wrong with you people! MY DAUGHTER IS DEAD!'"

"I imagined the scene I had just observed being replayed, this time with me in cuffs, my wife crying, my children screaming, the neighbors peeking out their windows, and the shame that would follow." A convicted drug smuggler for whom publicity was the harshest punishment reflects on the media's rush to judgment. He concludes that the spotlight often falls on the wrong cases, and that for every "Queen of Mean" found guilty "thousands of stories of injustice" remain unheard.

"White middle-America, those who consume around 70 or 80 percent of the illicit drugs taken in this country, can sit back in their living rooms and watch evening news visuals that 47 percent of the time show black people with drugs, even though African-Americans actually consume less than 20 percent of America's illegal substances." A novelist and former soldier in the "War on Drugs" argues that media coverage has sacrificed independence and objectivity for propaganda and infotainment.

"We exist in a day when the Bill of Rights has been virtually destroyed by a Supreme Court majority determined to reduce it to nothingness, insofar as the rights of criminal defendants are concerned," writes the author, founder of the Center for Constitutional Rights. But defense lawyers still have one avenue open to them—the press—which they must use "imaginatively and ingeniously" to fight for their clients' rights.

"When I sat on the bench I always wondered about any reporter I saw in my courtroom," says the author, a former judge *and* journalist. "Often I knew that the reporter had no idea of what I was doing, what the judicial system was about, what the language being used in the courtroom meant, and what rights were being protected and advanced through the legal system." Throw in Hollywood's version of justice, he says, and the result undermines the public's confidence in the criminal justice system as a whole.

The information officer for the Minnesota judiciary describes her work in easing communication between those two traditional adversaries, judges and reporters. "I am not a 'handler,'" she writes, "Neither am I a lawyer. My job is to make the courts work better by making sure the public understands what it is that judges do."

When she showed up at a murder scene with actor Kurt Russell in tow, the Pulitzer Prize-winning police reporter for the *Miami Herald* found that the crowd forgot about the corpses, the blood and the newly orphaned children. Suddenly murder didn't seem to matter much anymore.

Part III   The Culture of Crime

"'Naked City,' the classic New York cop series that ran on ABC from 1958 to 1963, had this famous signature: 'There are eight million stories in the naked city....' And now, as it turns out, there are eight million TV programs that tell them." So begins the Pulitzer Prize-winning television critic of the *Los Angeles Times,* who worries that prime-time television's preoccupation with violence fuels public panic and is an "abuse of the airwaves."

The number of American children held in public and private institutions rose steadily in the 1980s, despite the fact that the number of children in the population and the rate of youth arrests for serious crimes were both decreasing. "Why are more kids being locked up when fewer are being arrested? One reason is pressure from a public that believes juvenile crime is out of control," says the author, a civil rights reporter, and she questions the news media's neglect of a system that incarcerates nearly 100,000 children.

"Today, more than 65 percent of the women living in American cities are afraid to go out alone at night for fear of harm," writes a noted social scientist. The news media's coverage of sexual assault is at once salacious and inadequate, she argues, and particularly striking in the new age of soft news and infotainment. "Media executives seem to hold on to their belief that violence and crime sell, and to insist that stories about sex crimes against women sell best."

The *Associated Press Stylebook* defines an "automatic" as "a kind of pistol designed for automatic or semiautomatic firing." "How can a reporter make sense of that?" asks the author, the senior editor for legal affairs at *U.S. News & World Report,* and he goes on to cite several other examples of reportorial ineptitude when it comes to firearms. "America's news media," he charges, "consistently display a mixture of bias, carelessness and plain error in reporting issues involving guns."

"Because so much writing on the 'Wild West' has been meretricious, serious historians of the West have until recently avoided the entire subject of outlaws and gunfighters," writes the author, president of the Western History Association. In the absence of meaningful interpretation, there flourishes instead a "contradictory folklore of Western heroism, a narrative told first in newspapers, magazines and dime novels, and later by Hollywood, that reveals Americans' deep ambiguity about crime and justice."

The reigning patriarch of American crime fiction discusses the influences of journalism and Hollywood on his work, and what makes his criminals tick.

A deposition—the sworn written testimony of witnesses in a *civil* case. Criminal cases almost never include them, and that's just one of the reasons criminal cases are easier to cover, particularly for media outlets without the resources to do better. But "civil cases are where basic conflicts in our society are resolved," writes the author, a lawyer and reporter, "and many are as fascinating as anything in criminal court or on 'L.A. Law.'"

The tradition of Russian crime reporting began with Dostoyevsky, was influenced by more factual "European" approaches, twisted by Communist ideology, and then unleashed by glasnost. "For generations the Soviet people were told that crime just did not belong to the society of the proletariat," writes a Russian columnist for *Newsweek*. Now, "a form of reporting that was virtually nonexistent for 50 years occupies the prize place in every major newspaper and on every TV channel."

Part IV   Review Essay

A historian reviews the work of five generations of New York City crime reporters and shows how little—and how much—has changed about the beat and those who cover it. "They titillate with sex and violence, astound with explorations of the inner city, and warn of what to fear on a walk down a dark side street. Then they depart—leaving readers thrilled, frightened, confused and scarcely more knowledgeable about why crimes exist and what they can do about them."

Preface

For generations, critics of the press have had one consistent complaint: too much crime in the news. As they decry the emphasis on the lurid and the sensational, they keep coming back to crime, saying that it is the essence of "bad" news and is largely responsible for the negative slant of the press on almost everything. Serious students of news agree that news does have a negative coloration and that the media's historic love affair with crime, criminals and criminal behavior is largely responsible. At the same time, media scholar Harold Lasswell argues that one of the principal functions of the mass media is "surveillance of the environment," which means giving people clues about the nature of the communities in which they live and whether or not they are safe.

One of the earliest collections of newspaper reportage, John Wight's *Mornings at Bow Street* (1824), provided a glimpse of the English courts as they adjudicated disputes, many of them involving crimes great and small. In America, the growth of crime coverage coincided with the penny press of the 1830s. These popular newspapers were sold to the masses for a single penny and often contained accounts of crimes ranging from murder to petty theft. The publishers believed, and rightly, that ordinary people would be more interested in crime than in high finance or foreign policy. Crime or unlawful activity was thought to be more immediate and closer to people's daily lives than the pronouncements of a foreign minister, for example. With the growth of cities, crime in America, at least, became more rampant and more vital to people's existence, although one could argue that the press's preoccupation with crime conditioned the public to expect a violent society and perhaps even made people believe that life was more dangerous than it actually was.

Crime and criminal activity are linked to the function of criminal law, which has been defined by the *Directory of the Social Sciences* as follows:

> to preserve public order and decency, to protect the citizen from what is offensive or injurious, and to provide sufficient safeguards against exploitation and corrup-

tion of others, particularly those who are specially vulnerable because they are young, weak in body or mind, inexperienced, or in a state of special physical, official or economic dependence.

At the same time, crime has helped shape the modern definition of news, because news usually involves conflict and whatever is bizarre, sensational or deviant; and crime clearly is deviant behavior.

Crime is a staple of the modern media, as shown by the attention given to celebrated trials involving famous people. For example, one of the most seminal trials that shaped news coverage (and media criticism) was that of Bruno Richard Hauptmann, who was tried and convicted of kidnapping and murdering the son of aviator Charles Lindbergh in the 1930s. In the 1950s, the trial of Dr. Samuel H. Sheppard, an osteopath in Cleveland, Ohio, similarly rode on a wave of sensational reporting, much of it later deemed deleterious by critics and courts alike. That trial, along with one that never occurred—that of Lee Harvey Oswald, who was accused of assassinating President John F. Kennedy but killed within hours of his arrest—led to a national discussion of the issue of press versus fair trial, pitting the rights of the media and the public under the First Amendment against those of the defendant under the Sixth Amendment to the Constitution of the United States. Again, after much hand-wringing, codes of conduct for court officers and journalists were agreed upon, and more than 30 states organized fair trial-free press committees.

While most of the constraints on the media were voluntary for a time, the rules seemed to work pretty well. Still, First Amendment attorneys worried that even voluntary rules could be made mandatory by courts if they chose to define appropriate and proper journalistic standards. In time, that is exactly what happened, and the genteel agreements among court officers, lawyers and journalists broke down by the early 1980s.

Then in 1994, what may be the most celebrated criminal case in modern American history emerged when former football star, actor and television personality O.J. Simpson was accused of murdering his ex-wife, Nicole, and her friend, Ronald Goldman. Massive media coverage preempted even soap operas, and the nation was captivated. In an age when TV cameras are allowed in most trial courtrooms, the public got both a close look at legal proceedings and considerably more feedback from reports outside the courtroom. Tabloid sensationalism about the case mounted, causing the judge in the case, Lance Ito, to try to shield potential jurors from what he thought was contaminating publicity.

Today, some critics assert that the media system is out of control and that courts and laws are unable to influence how they and their activities are perceived in society. This is probably true, but at the same time, the principle of open courtrooms and freely accessible information seems to take precedence over constraints on the media. And it also might be argued that even in the O.J. Simpson case, it was possible for discerning readers and viewers to get a wide range of high-quality information, as well as the more scurrilous and sensational.

What the O.J. Simpson case indicated, though, was the durability and continuing importance of crime coverage in America and elsewhere. Crime is a topic of universal appeal and ultimately makes a statement about the nature of the society itself. In the 1990s, however, it became clear that media coverage of crime was often misleading not in detailing specific cases but in giving the overall impression that crime was on the rise when, in fact, various statistics indicated that the number of violent crimes actually decreased in many metropolitan areas. Crime is often the focal point of elections and politics, with office seekers arguing that they will be tougher on crime than their opponents will. Covered without context, such claims often cloud full public understanding of crime and criminal activity.

Crime coverage largely focuses on individual crimes and how society copes with them. This involves victims and defendants, prosecutors and defense attorneys, witnesses and judges and, of course, the jury. Beyond this, there are other experts on crime, such as criminologists, sociologists and forensic psychiatrists and, additionally, historians and public affairs analysts. Because the problem of crime is so important, what people actually think about it is critical to understanding and covering the story.

Historians of the press point to some improvements in the range, scope and quality of crime reporting and the re-creation of the crime story. No media outlet has been more riveted on this than the cable channel Court TV, which covers a wide range of trials and legal-social issues 24 hours a day. That such a service could even exist speaks volumes about the American people's interest in and fascination with crime.

This book is produced not to foster pedestrian coverage of crime as it has historically been done but rather to suggest that there is something that can be learned from a nexus of those directly involved with criminal proceedings or processes and journalists and scholars. All too often, the crime story is told by journalists who draw almost exclusively on first-hand and self-serving sources. Less often do they seek explanation and interpretation from other experts, such as sociologists, historians or theologians. They ought to, if the best intelligence about crime is to be made available to the public through the media. Our goal here is to lay out the problem and engage voices from media, scholarship and the inner world of the crime story in order to suggest some resolutions and understanding.

As always, the editors are grateful to Irving Louis Horowitz, who edits this series, and to members of our staff who helped along the way, especially Lisa DeLisle, associate editor of the *Media Studies Journal.* What began as an issue of this *Journal* was edited, reworked and augmented to produce this book which we hope will be illuminating to readers from journalism and the social sciences as well as from related fields.

> Everette E. Dennis
> Executive Director
> The Freedom Forum Media Studies Center
> Columbia University
> New York City
> February 1995

Introduction

There is no journalistic work more deserving of the designation "story" than news of crime. From antiquity, stories of crime have been about the human condition, and whether the tale comes from Homer, Hollywood or the city desk, it is at bottom about the human capacity for cruelty and suffering; about desperation and fear; about sex, race and public morals. Facts are important to the telling of a crime story, but ultimately less so than the often apocryphal narratives we derive from them.

Crime is also the most common and least studied staple of news. Its prominence dates at least to the 1830s, when the urban penny press employed violence, sex and scandal to build dizzying new levels of circulation and begin the modern age of mass media. In its coverage of crime, in particular, the penny press represented a new kind of journalism, if not a new definition of news, that made available for public consumption whole areas of social and private life that the mercantile and political press had theretofore ignored.

In the latter half of the 20th century, the reach of mass communication, combined with the visual impact of photojournalism and television, forced journalists to consider other aspects of crime news, particularly the conflict between the constitutional requirements of a free press and the right to a fair trial. This conflict reached its peak in the mid-1960s, when in the span of a few years the Warren Report on the assassination of President Kennedy, several U.S. Supreme Court decisions, and the recommendations of the American Bar Association's Reardon Report on Fair Trial and Free Press all found serious fault with press coverage of criminal matters and recommended, among other things, that judges control journalists with gag orders and enforce them with the threat of contempt. Thus threatened, journalists in several states voluntarily formed cooperative agreements with their state judiciary, and by 1970 more than 30 states had so-called "bench-bar-press committees." Throughout the 1970s, however, the news media's legal right of access to judicial proceedings became more certain, and by 1980, when the U.S. Supreme Court established the right to attend trials in *Richmond Newspapers v. Virginia,* these cooperative ventures had begun to decline.

Today few such bench-bar-press organizations remain, and those that do are not very active. For many the death knell came with a 1981 Washington Supreme Court case, *Federated Publications v. Swedberg,* which upheld a trial judge's order that compelled journalists attending a pretrial hearing to abide by the Washington's bench-bar-press guidelines. *Swedberg* was less a legal milestone than it was an unfortunate incident—in 1975 Justice Harry Blackmun had said in *Nebraska Press Association v. Stuart* that voluntary guidelines were too vague to survive constitutional scrutiny as part of a judicial order—but it nonetheless prompted several other states' bench-bar-press organizations to dissolve or amend their guidelines.

Journalism students who study crime coverage usually do so in this legal context, in which *Swedberg* is an outpost of the inquiry. They will also examine crime news in courses on public affairs reporting, where they are frequently taught the old and admirable rules about avoiding prejudicial information and defamatory statements, as well as the ethical issues surrounding coverage of victims and their families.

What they frequently do not learn is how news of crime and coverage of the police beat figure into news decisions. Neither do they encounter any of the criminology literature on media and crime, which observes virtually as principle that crimes receive news coverage according to public perception of their gravity, and thus in obverse proportion to their frequency. Instances of violent crime—murder, for example—are tiny compared to the other categories of crime that criminologists recognize—property crime, vice, organized crime, for example—but they constitute the bulk of crime stories in newspapers and on television.

Many of these same students will later work the police beat, where news organizations often break in new hires, and only then will they be forced to reconcile their legal and ethical training with their intuitive understanding of crime's value as a news story. The resulting clash of values creates news coverage that diminishes many serious crimes while it exults over lesser ones, and a pattern of coverage that is either mind-numbingly routine or that flirts with the sensational.

Media critics who decry this state of affairs rush too quickly to judgment: the infrequency and horror of violent crime in particular are the essence of "newsworthiness," at once fascinating and repulsive for audiences and journalists alike. Crime stories are both news *and* drama, and to ignore either is to diminish the other. The best crime reporters have always known this, and the worst have found countless opportunities to exploit it.

At the same time it is apparent that this practiced cognitive dissonance in crime coverage has resulted in some serious, if unintended, problems. For example, those who are most often victims of crime—the urban poor, many of them people of color—become fillers in the metro pages, while those whose experience with crime is least—middle- and upper-class whites—receive the most extensive coverage as victims precisely because of their statistical misfortune. In the end the cosmology of crime created in the media is both defined and distorted by issues of race, class and ethnicity, a result that all too often has unfortunate consequences for public life and public policy.

Many media commentators say that if crime news has changed at all in recent years it has become more pervasive. As consultant Lee Hanna has noted, anyone who watches local television news today is bombarded with tales of violence and mayhem; and crime and police news, often in the form of docudrama, has become a cheap and plentiful staple of prime-time television, just as it once was for the pioneers of the penny press. In a time of shrinking audiences and dwindling advertising revenues, crime news is easy to gather and promote. Unfortunately, crime stories are rarely covered in any sort of meaningful context and typically exclude, for example, how cases proceed through the criminal justice system.

But for all the roar of guns and gore, it's not at all clear what the impact is on public beliefs and attitudes, which, with crime as in other areas, defy easy cause-and-effect generalizations. Neither is it certain that this glut of information is in the least harmful to the exercise of criminal justice. In its own way, even in the most celebrated cases, news coverage is likely to be journalistically balanced, however sensational. Knowing this, good prosecutors and defense attorneys have made strategic use of the news media part of their professional repertoire, and they have learned to adapt their clients' tales, the public's moral and civic outrage, to the demands of the news and entertainment marketplace. In such circumstances the ideal of the impartial juror has been tainted with the reality of the ignorant one, and in recent years several legal scholars have questioned whether people who are frighteningly unaware of public affairs really make better jurors than those who are participants in the information age.

The introductory section to this volume, led by American studies scholar Elliott Gorn, attempts to place crime reporting into its historical and cultural perspective. In his essay "The Wicked World: The *National Police Gazette* and Gilded-Age America," Gorn looks at the legendary and hugely successful 19th-century journal of sex, sports and violence and its flamboyant editor, Richard Kyle Fox. Printed on pink paper, the *National Police Gazette* horrified Victorian society and New York's elite press, and even made the penny press seem urbane. But Fox and the *Gazette* were also visionary, staging "pseudoevents" like water-drinking contests and devoting lavish illustration to the bizarre and the bloody.

The "cosmology of fear" in which Richard Kyle Fox made his fortune has been a reliable source of news ever since. But the media are a part of that cosmology, says Hunter College sociologist Steven Gorelick, not merely its creators. Certainly the media's obsession with violent crime turns statistical data inside out, he argues, but he asks of the reader what one editor asked him: "How would *you* cover it?" Gorelick's answer: "If you're going to be sensational, be sensational, be explicit, pull no punches, leave no doubts, forget the euphemisms. Don't make the story palatable. The real story usually isn't, and readers should know that."

David Simon, the police reporter for the *Baltimore Sun,* agrees. The author of *Homicide: A Year on the Killing Streets,* Simon argues that conventional crime reporting is routine and anesthetizing, "the very essence of what journalism should not be," and he reacquaints the reader with the great narrative crime reporters of an earlier time and the world of pain and suffering that they brought home to their readers.

The second section of the book offers a selection of highly personal views on media and crime from people whose experience, in many cases, came at a high price. New Yorker Ellen Levin recounts the shock of being forced into the public spotlight when her daughter was murdered in Central Park in 1986. Following her, an ex-convict for whom publicity was the harshest punishment reflects on the media's rush to judgment and notes that for every high-profile criminal case there are "thousands of stories of injustice" that go untold; and Kim Wozencraft, a former undercover narcotics officer, now a novelist, talks about the media's willing participation in the politics and propaganda of the "War on Drugs."

Three chapters then take a closer look at the media's interaction with criminal justice, beginning with "A Chill Wind Blows," by attorney William Kunstler, who argues that in a judicial climate hostile to defendants' rights the skillful use of the press is about all that remains of a defense attorney's arsenal. Thomas Hodson, a former trial judge in Athens, Ohio, laments the prime-time mentality that dominates news and entertainment treatment of the criminal justice system, outlining an adversarial view of bench-press relations that Minnesota court information officer Rebecca Fanning makes a living trying to dispel.

Closing the section is a vignette on murder and mayhem in Miami by Pulitzer Prize-winning police reporter Edna Buchanan, who offers a numbing tale about violent crime in an age of celebrity.

The book's final section, "The Culture of Crime," is a mix of views on crime in American media, beginning with Howard Rosenberg's "Nervous in the Naked City." Rosenberg, TV critic for the *Los Angeles Times,* notes that where once there were "'eight million stories in the naked city,' now there are eight million TV programs that tell them." The next two chapters examine children and women, respectively, two groups that figure prominently in crime portrayals. Civil rights reporter Michele Magar examines the largely uncovered juvenile justice system in "Kids and Crime"; and University of Washington sociologist Margaret Gordon looks at news coverage of rape in "The Female Fear."

American crime is symbolized by the gun, of course, but according to *U.S. News & World Report* Senior Editor Ted Gest, most reporters wouldn't know a semiautomatic from a salami sandwich. Moreover, Gest says in "Firearms Follies," they wouldn't care—since most are heavily biased in favor of gun control to begin with. Following him, historian Richard Brown of the University of Oregon looks at the conflicting mythologies Americans cherish about crime and justice in "Desperadoes and Lawmen: The Folk Hero"; and in "Making a Killing: An Interview with Elmore Leonard," the reigning patriarch of American crime fiction discusses the influences of journalism and Hollywood on his work, and what makes his criminals tick.

Closing this section of the book are two "outside" views, the first from journalist and lawyer Peter Levin, who, in "You Want Me to Read a What?" muses on the fact that criminal cases get far more press attention than civil ones do, even though "civil cases are where basic conflicts in society are resolved." *Newsweek* columnist Alexei Izyumov then looks at the long tradition of Russian crime reporting, from Fyodor Dostoyevsky to the new age of post-putsch sensationalism. "For generations Soviet people were told that crime just did not belong to the society of the proletariat," Izyumov writes, but today the crime beat is a flourishing part of a new and increasingly competitive media system.

Finally, historian Robert Snyder writes a book review, "Glimpses of Gotham," in which he examines the work of five generations of New York City crime reporters. "At the heart of crime reporting lies a massive irony," Snyder says: "Although crime news usually means fast-breaking daily stories, the practices, purposes and postures of American crime reporting have remained largely unchanged for more than 150 years. With all the changes in news organizations and technology, their craft remains the same."

The Editors

I

Overview

1

The Wicked World:
The National Police Gazette and
Gilded-Age America

Elliott J. Gorn

Sensational news reports of crime and corruption, warned Anthony Comstock, were destroying America's youth: "They make a pure mind almost impossible. They open the way for the grossest evils. Foul thoughts are the precursors of foul actions." Comstock wrote during the heroic age of capitalist expansion in the late-19th century, an era that coincided with an easing of rigid Victorian ways. The thaw in morality disturbed many respectable Americans. Let down the floodgates to passion just a bit, clergymen, editors and reformers warned, and the tide of lust would wash away virtue. The reign of sin, of hedonism, of self-indulgence had already begun, and evidence was everywhere—in crime, in pornographic literature, in high living and extravagant consumption, in gambling and prostitution. The loosening of standards was particularly evident in the lower wards of Manhattan, where tens of thousands of working-class men and women—individuals living beyond the watchful eyes of moral agents such as churches, shopkeepers and kin—reveled by night.

For those who sniffed foulness at the wellsprings of virtue, the printed words flooding the country in the last decades of the century were a constant source of anxiety: "The father looks over his paper in the morning to ascertain the state of the market, to inform himself as to the news of the day," mused Comstock, founder and secretary of the New York Society for the Suppression of Vice, in his 1883 book *Traps for the Young*. "His attention is attracted by the heavy headlines designed to call especial attention to some disgusting detail of crime.... He turns away in disgust, and thoughtlessly throws down in the library or parlor, within reach of his children, this hateful, debauching article, and goes off to business little thinking that what he thus turns from his child will read with avidity."

Detailed and sensational news stories about wickedness, according to Comstock, glamorized the lives of libertines, harlots and criminals, and destroyed parents' best efforts at sheltering their children: "This deadly stream thus poured in to thousands of homes is breeding scoffers and breaking down the restraints and counteracting the sweet influences of religion." Even worse than newspapers, Comstock believed, illustrated weeklies concentrated evil messages into a single source, so that rather than occasional sensational stories scattered amidst news and business reports, the depravity was undiluted. Add illustrations, and "we then have a thing so foul that no child can look upon it and be as pure afterward." Such publications unleashed passions so strong that the quiet piety and self-restraint necessary to lead useful lives became impossible.

Comstock's name evokes snickers today, but late-19th century America honored and respected him. His New York Society was supported and bankrolled by a powerful group of socially prominent men— J.P. Morgan (finance), William E. Dodge (copper), Samuel Colgate (soap, appropriately), Kilaen Van Rensselaer (of the old New York Dutch aristocracy), William C. Beecher (attorney and son of Henry Ward Beecher) and Morris Ketchum (merchant, banker, multimillionaire). Such men were agents of America's transformation, for they built corporations that gave rise to mass immigration, unimagined concentrations of wealth, ever-finer specialization of labor, and bureaucracies employing a whole new class of white-collar workers. But even as their efforts caused radical change, they lamented the lost world of their youth. Unruly and heterogeneous cities were quite unlike the small towns and farms of romanticized antebellum childhoods.

The anti-vice campaign was an effort by reformers to patch up the cracks on the cultural edifice. Piety, hard work, sobriety, steady habits, frugality; a strict division of sexual roles into home, nurturance and moral elevation for women; work, productivity and patriarchal authority for men; above all, tight control of bodily desires and the checking of all forms of lust—these were the central virtues. It was, of course, a bourgeois culture, a culture that at once facilitated, sanctified and set moral limits on the process of acquiring property, building businesses and consolidating fortunes.

Above all, Comstock and his allies believed that evil was a contagion and that unregulated freedom of the press allowed the disease to spread. Comstock called on parents to keep "vile and crime-full illustrated papers" out of their homes and to boycott stores that sold them. By glamorizing the fast life, illustrated weeklies made the Victorian virtues of piety, morality and steady habits seem dull. Why labor diligently when easy money, sexual adventure and good times were there for the taking?

Undoubtedly the most popular and influential of these salacious publications—and certainly one uppermost in Comstock's mind, one that he took to court on several occasions—was the *National Police Gazette.* The "barber's bible" was kept on file at saloons, hotels, liveries, barber shops—anywhere men (for it was very much a journal aimed at a male audience) congregated—so that circulation estimates of 150,000 copies per week seriously underrepresent its readership. In the very year that Comstock published *Traps for the Young,* the new *Police Gazette* tower at the foot of the Brooklyn Bridge was one of the most noteworthy buildings on the New York skyline, and the journal's owner was well on his way to becoming a multimillionaire.

No doubt the *Gazette*'s success by the late 1870s and early 1880s through coverage of "human interest" stories—crime, sexual scandals, corruption, sports, glamour, show business—set an example for the daily papers. By the 1890s, the "new journalism" practiced by the burgeoning dailies packaged the news as a series of melodramas and atrocities, of titillating events covered as spectacles, complete with illustrations. If, as Michael Schudson observes, men like William Randolph Hearst and Joseph Pulitzer redefined news reporting as the art of storytelling, of entertainment with words and pictures, the *National Police Gazette* led the way for them, pioneering the techniques that later gave rise to the "yellow press."

The *Gazette* began publication in 1845 as a chronicle of the crimes of the day, though in its early years the weekly did more than merely report on malefactors and their wrongdoings. The *Gazette* was very much an organ of artisan and working-class culture, upholding the virtues of natural rights, republicanism and the public good, condemning not only those who committed crimes against individuals and their property, but also corrupt public officials, all who held inordinate economic power, and all who sought "aristocratic" privilege. So persistent in exposing transgressors was the early *Police Gazette* that editor George Wilkes and his cohorts found themselves in numerous brawls, some of them resulting in fatalities.

By the Civil War, however, the implicit assumption that scoundrels of wealth and power were as culpable as horse thieves and pickpockets got lost in more conventional crime reporting. During the war the *Gazette* turned from covering government corruption to publishing lists of Union soldiers absent without leave in order to help the federal Army stem the tide of desertions. In the postbellum period, George Matsell, former New York City chief of police, took over the paper and began sensationalizing the coverage of crime, but despite his efforts circulation dwindled, and as the century entered its last quarter the *Gazette* teetered on extinction.

Enter Richard Kyle Fox, a Belfast journalist who had immigrated to America a year after Anthony Comstock had spearheaded the formation of the New York Society for the Suppression of Vice. Upon his arrival in the States Fox went to work for the New York *Commercial Bulletin,* but within two years he acquired the old *Police Gazette* in lieu of debts owed to him by the paper's owners.

Through the remainder of the 1870s Fox continued to emphasize crime but made some significant changes. He cut the size of the pages but increased their number to 16. Above all, he gave ever more space to illustrations, making them much more graphic depictions of murders, seductions and horrible accidents—all that was gruesome or thrilling. By 1883 Fox had worked out the formula that the *Police Gazette* followed for the remainder of the century. The end of the economic crisis of the 1870s and Fox's aggressive marketing (for example, he gave cut rates to hotels, saloons and barber shops, all of which kept back files for their male clientele) placed the *Gazette* among the top two dozen or so American magazines published in the quarter century following the Civil War. Special editions of the *Gazette*—especially those covering sporting events like championship fights—occasionally sold nearly half a million copies.

As with other newspapers and magazines of the era, advertising became an increasingly important source of the *Gazette*'s revenues. During the early 1880s the magazine contained a full page of advertisements, which were sold at 75 cents per line. Many of these ads were for Richard K. Fox publications, mostly compilations of stories previously printed in the *Police Gazette*. Other ads promoted sporting goods, saloons, vaudeville houses, venereal disease cures, organ-enlarging drugs, remedies for impotence, shoes, gambling aids, pictures of athletes and chorus girls and a variety of other goods. A few years later, advertising sold at $1 per line (the same rate as *Leslie's, Godey's* and *Ladies' Home Journal*), and two full pages of ads weekly filled Fox's coffers.

The tone of the *Gazette* was always personal, even chatty. Writers approached the reader as an equal, took him by the elbow, and showed him a thing or two. The emphasis on rumor and gossip, on story well told, lowered the barriers between the producers of the paper and its consumers. Victorian didacticism and moral certitude were absent from these pages. Editorial style rarely made claims for voracity based on superior knowledge; columns of jokes or tidbits of sporting information left little room for pontificating on the issues of the day.

Coverage of sports—especially illegal blood sports like boxing and cockfighting—of vaudeville and variety shows, and of sexual scandals, particularly among the socially prominent, grew increasingly important to the *Gazette,* but crimes of violence, the more bizarre and blood-soaked the better, were the journal's lifeblood during the 1870s and '80s. By the late 1870s the *Gazette* was printed on pink paper, and its graphic displays of blood and sex far outstripped any other publication. A regular column, "Vice's Varieties," offered brief descriptions of wrongdoing contributed by readers from every state. Series with more specific purposes were also important, and many had a historical cast. "Lives of the Poisoners: How They Killed and What They Killed With," written by "a member of the New York bar," gave detailed descriptions of celebrated murders committed with various toxins. The titles of other regular columns reveal the *Gazette*'s tone: "Murder and Suicide: A Gush of Gore and Shattering Brains All Around the Horizon"; "This Wicked World: A Few Samples of Man's Duplicity and Woman's Worse Than Weakness"; "Crooked Capers: Scrapes and Scandals of All Sorts and From All Quarters"; "Glimpses of Gotham" by Paul Prowler (a.k.a. Samuel MacKeever), which took readers on tours of the slums and dives and resorts of the metropolis, giving them the vicarious excitement of participating in lives of deviance. Other ongoing summaries of crime around the nation went under such titles as "Homicidal Horrors," "Noose Notes" and "Crimes of the Clergy" (one of Fox's favorite subjects).

Other stories went beyond purely interpersonal violence to hint at the social dimensions of aggression. The stories in a single issue of the *Gazette* (October 9, 1886) offer a good example. One told of a Mrs. Pauline Mittelstaedt, who brought pregnant women into her lying-in hospital and then disposed of the infants for a fee of $300. An article about a Brooklyn "lunatic asylum" began with a description of how one inmate was murdered by an attendant with scalding water, and then went on to expose other horrors of the institution. Thus the headline—"Cooking a Cripple"—was followed by "How the Pauper Insane of the City of Churches are Housed and Maltreated Near Brooklyn." Another exposé described Georgia's convict lease system as one of pure exploitation by the state's wealthy to extract the labor of "ignorant negros and low whites" who died at rates approaching 20 percent per year. Implicitly, the *Gazette* here asked readers who the real criminals were.

Even coverage in the summer of 1884 of the death of the celebrated bank robber George Leonidis Leslie took on social overtones, for it was pointed out that Leslie was well educated, acted the gentleman, patronized the arts, theater and literature, and mixed with the best company. Again, who were the pillars of the community, who the scoundrels?

Sports slowly began to overtake crime and violence in the *Police Gazette*—Fox quickly learned the sales value of sports when coverage of the 1880 championship fight between Paddy Ryan and Joe Goss kept his presses rolling for days—so that by the late 1880s over half the written copy in most issues was devoted to games of physical competition. While some of this coverage went to comparatively mainstream sports like baseball (still a somewhat shady enterprise given its associations with gambling, drinking and other working-class vices) and college football, most of it dealt with sports that were criminal or violent or both. Boxing was illegal until 1892, and dreadfully bloody under the bare-knuckle rules. It was also the pet sport of the *Gazette*. Richard Kyle Fox decreed six weight classifications, offered championship belts in each, sponsored matches, put up stake money, fought anti-boxing laws in court, imported talent from abroad, arranged bouts in his offices and publicized upcoming events. He retained William Edgar Harding as his sports editor, and Harding wrote masterful accounts of prizefights. Indeed, sparring was not confined to the ring, as editor Fox exploited his personal enmity with fighter John L. Sullivan to back a series of challengers, whip up enthusiasm for the ring, and sell thousands of copies of his paper.

Not only boxing but cockfighting, ratting, dog baiting and other premodern blood sports received widespread coverage and sponsorship by the *Gazette*. So-called trash sports—such pseudo-events as "Battle of the Network Stars," activities with little basis in tradition but designed to attract television viewers—had their analogues in *Police Gazette* promotion and coverage of all sorts of bizarre competitions, water-drinking championships and hair-cutting contests among them. All of these events, from rifle shooting to six-day walking matches to weight lifting with one's teeth created instant celebrities because of publicity in the *Gazette*. Annie Oakley, for example, first came to national prominence when she won one of Richard Kyle Fox's contests for marksmanship.

Fox spent perhaps half a million dollars on belts, trophies, prizes and promotional expenses for these and other competitions, an investment that paid handsomely in increased sales of his paper. Along the way he provided an early model of a journal creating news, not merely reporting it. Since the goal of reporting was to entertain rather than enlighten citizens, why wait for events to happen? Through his sports pages, Fox blurred the line separating journalism from its subject matter, a hallmark of modern media.

If violence and sports were two pillars of the *Gazette* world, the third was sex. Virtually as soon as Fox took over as editor, nakedness increased, stories of infidelity proliferated and images of libidinous abandon multiplied. Many of these centered around the indiscretions of wealthy individuals or the hypocrisies of the devout. Samuel MacKeever described a rendezvous at a downtown department store in 1880 between two otherwise married people, both of substantial backgrounds. The man bought the woman an expensive coat, and MacKeever contrasted their moral and financial casualness with the poverty of the salesgirl who took their order. She smiled at her customers so as not to lose her job, which barely paid her enough to live. MacKeever concluded that shop girls in New York City were like the bond-girls of Constantinople, serfs amidst luxury, the "white slaves of the metropolis." Similarly, in a thoroughly typical story under the heading "Religious Notes," one Reverend Finerty of the Methodist Church of Mokona, Illinois, was accused of attempting an "outrage" against one of his flock. The clergyman slipped into her room and threw her down, but the young woman screamed, clawed his face, and freed herself.

Such stories had a double edge, at once upholding "female virtue" and exciting male readers with hints of its violation. The predominant image of women in the *Gazette*, however, was less concerned with protecting their honor and more with depicting them as free from Victorian strictures. Above all they were creatures of fantasy who openly gave and received pleasure. To give a seemingly innocuous example, a story from March 25, 1893, noted that a California woman sued for the right to attend horse races. The *Gazette* applauded the judge's decision to let her, noting that those who did not want to go should stay home, that choosing to attend such an event was the right of American citizens. Under the rubric of constitutional freedom, the *Gazette* here defended the right of the individual—whether male or female—to seek pleasure over the moral claims of the community.

Similarly, the journal was generally sensitive to the exploitation of women workers, particularly sexual exploitation by unscrupulous bosses. Yet in the leering way these stories were told and illustrated there was often a prurient, voyeuristic thrill at the exploitation of the powerless by the powerful. Indeed, the dominant theme once again was the right to pleasure, and ultimately this meant that women were valued for the sensuality they offered men. Thus there were countless depictions of free-and-easy chorus girls displaying their legs, barmaids tempting patrons and variety entertainers in lascivious poses. The sum total was soft-core pornography that presented women as objects of beauty to be possessed and, like champagne and cigarettes, consumed.

Far more disturbing were countless word or picture images associating women with violence. Many of these depicted women bloodying men; more commonly, it was women who received the damage, often at the hands of each other. Taken as a whole, the symbolism here is disturbing: Women were freed from the constraints of Victorian piety and domesticity only to become monsters, or to be victimized as the price of their freedom and "kept in their place" with violence. The inversion of roles in the *Gazette*—women played baseball, boxed, bicycled, committed crimes—means that we should not be surprised by representations of female violence here. But the images went beyond evenhanded androgyny. Just as the acknowledgment of female sensuality in the *Gazette*'s pages most often transformed women into objects of pleasure for men, representations of female bloodletting here became a pornography of violence for the benefit of male viewers.

But it was not only women who were kept in their place. Misogyny had its parallel in racism and anti-Semitism. For example, under the heading "An Invasion," the following appeared on August 5, 1882: "Talk about locusts, you fellows out West! You should be in New York. This year we have Jews and more Jews—whole shiploads of them. The Russians are a-rushin' things on us in the line of Hebrew goods. They are swamping everything. Locusts! You should just drop into this new Jerusalem and look at the noses that surround it. This isn't one Jew but a whole crowd of Jews. The sight would knock all the poetry out of Shakespeare or any other man."

In countless stories, the fascination with violence became singularly ugly with stories and pictures describing lynchings of black men who committed "outrages" against white women, an inherent trait of the race according to the *Gazette*. Eight drunken blacks allegedly entered a brothel in Mt. Vernon, Indiana, in October 1870. They pulled guns, "then huddled the girls in a room and, putting out the lights, inaugurated a beastly carnival, holding their pistols to the girls' heads and compelling them to submit to the loathsome embraces of all for an hour." All eight were shot, lynched or had their throats cut, restoring equilibrium. The Chinese, more devious and less virile than blacks, used drugs to get what they wanted, "luring even little girls into their dens in Mott Street and, after stupefying them with opium candy, debauching the poor creatures."

Racism and misogyny, however, were no bar to sympathy for the plight of white laborers and deep suspicion of the privileged. Such important strikes as Homestead and Patterson received considerable space in the *Gazette*'s pages, and workers were represented as aggrieved if not downright heroic, while owners tended to be shown as greedy and effete. Indeed, the *Gazette* revealed a world of undeserved privilege for a few and misery for the many. Stock speculators fleeced unsuspecting widows; businessmen seduced their employees; poverty tempted working girls into prostitution; clergymen stole from congregations; rich snobs expected others to pay their way in society; the wealthy viewed the poor as existing for their convenience. Judges, lawyers, doctors and businessmen were alternately heartless or incompetent, vultures or buffoons.

The *Gazette was* class-conscious in its way, populist to be more precise, but awareness of class did not lead to calls for rebellion. Again, the ethic of pleasure was foremost. Implicitly, the weekly message in countless tales of chorus girls and dance halls and spectator sports was that those who worked for wages in factories and offices should seek adventure, sensuality and exuberance in their leisure time in order to counter the ill effects of excessive labor. The *Police Gazette* would be their guide.

In trying to capture the essence of the *Police Gazette*, we need to keep in mind that it was, as it styled itself on its masthead, America's leading *illustrated* journal. I suspect that without pictures the *Gazette* would have attained nowhere near its popularity during the last quarter of the century. The front and back covers of every issue displayed full-page illustrations, and the total space devoted to pictures ranged from about one-quarter of the journal's 16 pages early in Fox's proprietorship to over half the total space—eight full pages plus vignettes scattered throughout written columns—by the mid-1880s. Illustrations were not aids to the printed word; on the contrary, many stories were doubtless selected for their graphic qualities, and written copy served as a guide to the images. The *Gazette* existed to display spectacles, to appeal to individuals' lusts, fears, hatreds, fantasies and desires with viscerally moving images that transformed the world's utter incomprehensibility into readily consumable visual information.

What are we to conclude about the *National Police Gazette*? Surely it was an important organ of New York City culture. While the *Gazette* saw itself as a national institution, most of its material came from New York, a sizable portion of its audience lived in or near the City, and it was very much a product of the fashions, the rhythms, the life of the town. But to understand the *Gazette* we need to be more precise about its readership. I suspect that a broad range of Americans occasionally and surreptitiously read the journal; the titillating stories and pictures no doubt appealed across boundaries of class, race and geography. But judging from what contemporaries thought of the journal, and from the ads and stories and illustrations in the weekly, the *Gazette* was above all the property of young white males of the working class and lower-middle class.

This large wage-earning class had appeared in the City before the last quarter of the 19th century, and earlier publications offered it some of the elements now in the *Police Gazette*. The original *Gazette* provided news about crime; the *Spirit of the Times* covered sports; the *Subterranean* bashed away at the rich and corrupt; *Frank Leslie's* illustrated the news of the day; and the New York *Herald* excited readers with scandalous stories. But none of these journals had available the mass wage-earning public Richard Kyle Fox discovered in Gilded-Age America, the techniques of production and distribution now at hand, nor the new entertainment business that provided so much of the *Gazette*'s copy.

Fox must have sensed the enormous new potential audience developing, an audience whose tastes his publication helped mold. The unreconstructed Victorian ethos did not well serve men who bore only its repressions and none of its rewards. The Gilded Age presented increasing numbers of workers with rigidly segmented realms of work and non-work time. Wage labor, whether blue-collar or white-collar, tended to be routine and highly specialized, offering little hope of advancement. As compensation, one might learn to seek pleasure in non-work hours, attending sports events, going to vaudeville shows, or even reading illustrated newspapers. The *Gazette* held out leisure as an alternative realm of fulfillment, a place where one could find excitement, at least vicariously. Moreover, sedentary work was hardly virile, and even factory laborers bent their efforts to the demands of managers and foremen, calling into question their own masculine independence. The *Gazette* modeled an alternative definition of masculinity, one centered on sports, saloons, life, violence, "loose" women or, more likely, the vicarious consumption of these.

The pleasures offered by the *Gazette* were not so much alternatives to the repressions of the workplace as compensations for its deprivations. Clearly, there was nothing inherently antithetical about labor activism and the joys of the flesh. In the *Gazette* the two coexisted on the same pages. While saloons and boxing matches and vaudeville shows probably did divert some men from more active involvement in politics, we must not lose sight of the cultural battlefield. Victorian mores were still largely intact for individuals standing at the centers of social and economic power during the last decades of the 19th century. If not workplace democracy, the ethos of the *Police Gazette* offered white working males a democracy of pleasure denied by Victorian culture. Here, at least, moral claims of those in authority were supplanted by workers' own "free" choices. Here too, glamour and excitement replaced workaday life.

But this bit of cultural democracy came at a high cost. After all, a world of consumer pleasure is a rather passive realm. More important, a disturbingly misanthropic ideology was inherent in the *Police Gazette*, and it becomes obvious not in any particular article or illustration, but in reading through year after year of the weekly. In a postwar era of Darwinism, corporate arrogance and government corruption, little on these pages was affirmed. If the journal was sometimes sympathetic to the cause of labor, it mainly was apolitical. Religion was never depicted as anything but hypocrisy. The wealthy were brazen and greedy—but at least they had the wherewithal to enjoy themselves. Women offered sensuality, but at best they were not to be taken seriously; at worst their sexuality invited male violence. Nonwhites were threatening, out of control in their lusts, but imagining the joy of their unbridled passions and the orgies of violence needed to check them provided dizzying fantasies of passions that had been excluded from daily life. On the pages of the *Gazette*, everyone was out for nothing more than his or her own enjoyment, and anyone claiming to seek anything more was a hypocrite.

Barely clearing the moral boundaries that allowed it to be mass produced and distributed, each week's issue resonated with all that remained deeply repressed by the cult of domesticity and by the capitalist workplace. Depicting a world of sexuality and violence and thrilling adventure, the *Gazette* attacked the legitimacy of Victorian culture even if it did nothing to change the social relationships that had fostered that culture. Seductions, mutilations and swindles were condemned on these pages, but they were described with such loving detail that voyeuristic gratification was the real agenda.

The world of the *Police Gazette* was not far from our own age, so fascinated with the manipulation of images, with spectacles. Rapes, scams, murders, extramarital affairs, drinking, carousing; even as the *Gazette* condemned these it made them the focus of its attention, made its readers question who were the real sinners and who the saints. Individuals who seemed most honest, solid and prosperous might be most corrupt. This was not the age of enterprise at all, but of posturing, role-playing, false appearances. Potentially a brilliant insight into Gilded-Age culture, Fox offered no call to reform, merely an invitation to play the game and have fun.

Anthony Comstock gave journals like the *Police Gazette* too much credit for polluting American life. Such cultural phenomena were symptoms of change as much as causes. Still, Comstock had a point. The moral universe he and his friends grew up in was beginning to fall apart. In the dawning age of gratification, of spectacles, of image production,

Richard Kyle Fox and his spiritual heirs helped set the cultural tone for the nation, shape its values, and amass fortunes along the way. If Comstock's Victorianism was a survival of an earlier era of entrepreneurial capitalism, Fox represented the new age of consumption. Historians ignore the *National Police Gazette* at their peril. Fox and his publication were at the vanguard, and the sensibility they represented, for better or worse, became a significant part of American life.

Elliott J. Gorn is director of the American Studies department at Miami University in Oxford, Ohio.

2

Cosmology of Fear

Steven Gorelick

One recent afternoon my 12-year-old son failed to come home by his usual 5 p.m. arrival time. I was worried. At 5:30 I called the place where he had had an after-school appointment, and he wasn't there.

I was horrified. I thought things I cannot even utter. Anyone who might have been with me at the time would have witnessed something close to a full-blown panic attack.

My son showed up at 6, and far from anything insidious, he had been at his school library doing homework. I was relieved. I was elated. I was shocked by my own reaction.

I was shocked because I know more than the average person what the most likely dangers to one's children are. Indeed, I spend a good portion of my academic life studying and trying to debunk the classic cultural images that people have about crimes against children. I am particularly interested in the life history that these images have in the press. There was an explosion of coverage in the mid-1980s, and now it seems to have disappeared. What led to the explosion? How was it covered while it was "hot"? And why did it disappear? Currently I'm doing a study of several reporters, particularly in Boston and New York, who have covered widely publicized cases of child abuse, and in the process I've gotten to know a fair amount about the relative incidence of crimes against children: abductions by strangers, custodial abductions, sexual abuse, physical abuse and maltreatment. One outstanding book on this topic, Joel Best's *Threatened Children,* looks at the whole period of the 1980s as one in which the press constructed an atmosphere of ubiquitous childhood perils. Not just the print press, but television, films, books.

23

Now that I've laid out my credentials, I can confess that while I was on the way to work this morning I still couldn't shake the residual feeling that maybe something bad had happened to my son. And then I remembered the dedication to Best's marvelous book: "For Eric and Ryan, whose father worries anyway." I realized how fundamental are some of our fears and anxieties, how impervious to change they are, and how futile it is to expect that a responsive press would not resonate the fears that people really have. But beyond that I realized how unfair it is, and over-simple as well, to indict the press as the sole purveyor of misinformation and sensationalism.

I will grant that sensationalism conflicts in many ways with another of the press's primary functions—to serve as an educator for responsible citizenship and for responsible policy-making. But at the same time I believe we should give up the kind of elite press criticism that scorns the sensational in news coverage. Rather we should admit that the sensational has its rightful place in the press, and that within that context the press could do a *better* job of being sensational. The most heinous crimes can and should be covered in ways that more appropriately serve the media's public education function.

One of the classic texts I use when I teach this subject is Walter Lippmann's *Public Opinion*. Lippmann, of course, was one of the 20th century's most important thinkers on how we form our perceptions of the world, and, as is well known, he describes in his book the pictures of the world that we form in our heads and that we use to make all sorts of decisions about how to live our lives—what we should be afraid of, what food we should eat, what kind of relationships we should have. Of course, because health, safety and survival are basic human concerns, it's no coincidence that many of these pictures have to do with issues of crime and violence.

I've always imagined that each of us uses these pictures to form a personal cosmology of fear. These cosmologies are very detailed, and they change all the time, but they tell us what we should regard as safe or dangerous, and so they affect our daily lives in very direct ways. At the same time, of course, the whole communications literature is rife with studies that fail to establish any such direct connection between exposure to media content and subsequent behavior. Consequently I am inclined to believe that a lot of this happens just below the level of awareness. Our cosmology of fear reformulates continuously as we perceive new threats and try simultaneously to incorporate new information that renders old threats harmless.

Part of that process underscores another point—that these cosmologies of fear are not entirely a private matter. We talk about them with neighbors, co-workers, friends. We hear public officials talk about them, and we often find out that we are united in a larger, shared cosmology of fear. If you doubt that, you need only look at what happens when our individual cosmologies coalesce into a powerful, vocal force.

Consider, for example, what happened to New York Mayor David Dinkins in 1990 when a Utah tourist named Brian Watkins was murdered in a subway gang attack on his family. The mayor's first reaction was to try to keep people calm, to point out that subway platforms and cars are actually safer than the streets above ground and that the statistics for many violent crime categories had recently declined. Otherwise Dinkins went about his business as usual, as if to reassure the alarmed city that there was no need to panic. But the Watkins murder came at the end of a summer during which the press had given emphatic coverage to accidental shootings of children, most of them black and Hispanic. The city's revulsion over the Watkins murder coalesced into a palpable force that no amount of official reassurance could quell.

Eventually it became clear that the Mayor's response would have to be of a magnitude commensurate with the public's fear, and so it was that 5,000 additional police officers were proposed as the magic solution. There were suggestions that perhaps fewer than 5,000 would suffice, and a few lonely voices observed that these new troops would not actually hit the streets for a long time. A few others even wondered aloud if violent crime had in fact gone up.

I'm sure that personally the mayor was as distraught by the horror of the Watkins murder as any other citizen. I also think he was absolutely justified in trying to calm the panic. But he paid a political price for his actions. The frenzy was so high at the time that anything short of joining it was taken by the public as official indifference. As a researcher and a teacher, I know how perilous it is to claim a direct link between press coverage, public fear and public policy, but the Watkins case provides an interesting, intuitive case study of how these things work. Even if the local press were not pushing the magic 5,000 as an explicit agenda item— and I don't believe they were—simply reporting the panic as it pushed forward had a profound effect on the City's political leaders and their perceptions of public opinion.

The most comprehensive scholarly study about crime coverage and its impact on public opinion is Doris Graber's 1980 book *Crime News and the Public*. In Graber's study about 25 percent of the stories in newspapers are about crime; and 95 percent of her respondents say the mass media are their main source of information about crime and justice.

After further analysis, Graber argues that media coverage of crime distorts the nature and frequency of crime. Other scholars and pundits have argued that it causes panics like the one that followed the Watkins murder, and that crime coverage overemphasizes the unusual and the sensational.

I'm not going to deny that crime coverage and the pictures we form in our heads are often very distorted versions of the world. Most of the studies that have looked at news coverage of crime—including my own—have come up with findings similar to Graber's. As a percentage of all reported crime, for example, murders are extremely unusual, and yet they represent as much as 50 percent of the crimes covered in newspapers. Burglaries—both residential and nonresidential—are a relatively significant portion of all reported crime but are virtually invisible in press coverage. Motor vehicle theft is a growing national epidemic—and in some cities it accounts for as much as 20 percent of reported crime—yet it, too, is nearly invisible in press coverage. These distortions come up again and again in studies of urban media (less so in rural media, where rote listings of police reports are still common), and they are often cited as the cause of a virtual social paralysis among significant segments of the population.

But I'd like to suggest that it is simply unfair to dismiss the press as a purveyor of misinformation, or to blame the media for our fear of crime.

First, there is very good evidence that people don't automatically adopt the version of crime that is depicted in the press. The best work that I know on this subject is by criminologist Mark Warrs of the University of Texas at Austin, who has done ground-breaking studies of how the fear of crime actually works, what people are really afraid of, and what the components of fear are.

Warr defines the fear of crime as a combination of two factors: the extent to which people perceive a crime as serious, and the extent to which they perceive themselves to be at risk for it. He finds that although people might perceive a crime as serious, residual folk wisdom leads them not to perceive themselves at risk of it. He has shown, for example, that murder is far from the most feared crime even though people constantly rate it among the most serious crimes.

In fact, using Warr's definition of the fear of crime, the crime people fear most is having someone break into their house while they are away. His studies also show that residential burglary is especially fearful for women because they often associate it with other crimes, such as rape or murder. The point is that people are smarter, more resilient and more resourceful than the automatons whose cosmologies are supposedly buffeted around by media reports of heinous crimes.

Other researchers have also found that people adopt views of crime other than those depicted in the press. Graber's study, for example, shows that the media often ignore the social or economic context in which a crime occurs; yet hers and a number of other studies have shown that people do not accept crime news uncritically. Most are very willing to grant that economic deprivation can be a cause of crime. In 1982, for example, I did a study of the New York *Daily News* during a three-month period when the paper declared its own war on crime. One of the things I did was read the letters to the editor that the paper received, and while I might have expected to find letters urging all manner of physical torture and punishment for your run-of-the-mill street criminal, I found instead a surprising residue of compassion and understanding of the complexity of crime.

The point I'm trying to make is that the media do not create our fears of crime, *rather they share their own fears and reproduce ours*. Perhaps the point seems obvious, but think for a moment about what it means for press coverage. I was forced to do so recently when I interviewed the deputy managing editor of a prestigious metropolitan daily about an incident of child sexual abuse that had taken place in the area that the paper covered. The case had received almost daily coverage for three or four years, and I asked him the typical press critic's question: Wasn't he concerned that the focus on such cases diverted attention from the perils that children are more likely to face? Wasn't he concerned, for example, that the incredible play his paper gave to a case of child sexual abuse in daycare had greatly overstated the risk of such abuse while it obscured the more prevalent incidence of abuse in other settings? The editor's face reddened as he heard this almost boilerplate criticism of how the press covers social issues, and he answered with a question for me: "How would *you* have covered it?" Or would I have covered it at all?

At that moment I realized that I would have been out there hustling with everybody else, and I saw the dilemma that editors and reporters face every day. Our fascination with the unusual conflicts with the classic educational mission of the press, but the unusual and the sensational are wrapped up in the very definition of news. Indeed, fascination with the sensational is so deeply ingrained in individuals and in the larger culture that no one can avoid it. It has a place. It speaks to some of our most basic fears and anxieties, and in a strange way it also helps us feel safe. It enables us to enjoy, however mistakenly, the feeling that such things happen to them, not us.

I know, for example, that stranger abductions are rare. Yet I want to read the *New York Times'* coverage about the disappearance of Jacob Wetterling—a young Midwestern boy who was abducted apparently by a stranger two years ago and who has never been found. I know this kind of thing is rare, but I want to read about it. I'm a parent, and what parents haven't thought about something like this happening to their own children? In some ways, I think, news allows people to play out in fantasy a pent-up psychic energy that has few other outlets.

Anyone who claims that this kind of fascination with the unusual and the sensational is horrible and immoral denies human history and the nature of mythology. Think of Sophocles' Oedipus, who kills his father and marries his mother. Is patricide a typical crime? Of course not, but the fascination with patricide persists. Several years ago a young Asian woman in California drowned her two children in the surf. It was later established that she had done so after her husband had abandoned her. Infanticide isn't an epidemic problem in the United States, but who can say that reading about that incident is inherently less worthy than watching a production of Euripides' *Medea*?

Even without the economic imperative to which critics so readily ascribe such stories (i.e., sensationalism sells papers), these things should have a place and even be valued in news content. In fact, I think we should enjoy it; we should relish it; we should understand our own hunger for it; we should understand the ways that it often resonates with our most basic fears and anxieties; and we should use it to teach us about what we are afraid of. Those elitists who smirk at people who buy the *National Enquirer* while they lap up their own particular social class's version of the unusual and scandalous should come down from their high horse.

My wife is a theater director and a critic, and recently she took me to see a production of Euripides' *The Bacchae,* a play that features a mother who beheads and mutilates her own son. As I watched, I couldn't help but remember the *New York Post* editor who entered the headline writer's pantheon when he came up with "Headless Body in Topless Bar." I was struck by the persistence of some fascinations.

Moreover I refuse to believe that the story of the dismemberment, beheading and mutilation in *The Bacchae,* even though it speaks to a nobler part of the human intellect, is so very different from a story in the *New York Post* about a beheading in a bar. They both address basic human preoccupations, and I'm tired of patronizing dismissals of that reality. It is as useless and naive to suggest that the press should give less play to the sensational as it is to deny the innate impulses of the libido or of hunger. The sensational is deeply ingrained in our psyches; it speaks to our most basic fears and anxieties. The question for the press, and for the public, should be how to best serve this fundamental need.

For starters, I think we should give up completely the canonical demand that the press give less emphasis to the sensational and the unusual. There are other ways that the press can curb its worst excesses of scandal and distortion to better educate the public within a news environment in which the sensational will always have strong appeal.

First, I would suggest that the press be *more* explicit and *more* sensational. Stop with the euphemisms; leave no doubts about what happened.

Let me offer an example from what I have learned in studying press coverage of child sexual abuse. Many of these are horrible crimes, and I am familiar with cases where people have been convicted of crimes that are almost too horrible to discuss. But therein lies the problem: *They are almost too horrible to discuss.* I have trouble sitting here now writing about them. In the mid-1980s, when press coverage of these cases exploded, many newspapers and television stations relied on euphemisms for sexual organs and sexual acts, to gloss over the grisly acts that had been committed against these children. Sometimes it wasn't clear at all what had happened. "Sodomy," for example, can mean several things.

Another example: One of my favorite reporters at a large metropolitan newspaper told me a story about a motorboating accident involving alcohol in which a young woman was beheaded. The press reported the accident but not how the woman was killed, leaving the true horror of the accident unspoken. I don't think this educates well, or that it reflects well on a responsible press. If people get beheaded in motorboat accidents because of alcohol, I think the public needs to know that. If some people rape children, I think the public needs to know exactly what they do.

Be sensational, be explicit, pull no punches, leave no doubts, forget the euphemisms. If body parts are involved, tell us which body parts. Readers and viewers might be offended by more detailed discussions of some crimes, but that's no excuse. This *does not* mean that the Eye-witness Crew should pursue ever more blood-soaked video for the 11 o'clock teaser; rather that journalists, whatever their medium, should *explain* the real horror of these crimes. I think people want to know, and people need to know, even if they don't want to. In other words, if you're going to be sensational, be responsibly sensational. Be clear. Don't make the story palatable. The real story usually isn't, and readers should know that.

Secondly, I would urge reporters and editors to think about how an unusual or sensational story might be a manifestation of some larger social problem.

This sounds so obvious that I'm sure it insults some reporters, and indeed many reporters do try to do this when they say that a given crime is just "the tip of the iceberg" and offer a few statistics about how the incidence of that crime is actually increasing. But that's not what I'm talking about.

The trick here, and the challenge for the reporters, is to look for ways to report how an individual crime might point to a larger social problem without automatically implying that the incidence of the particular crime is on the rise.

I'll give you one example. Every expert knows that sexual abuse in families is overwhelmingly more frequent than abuse that takes place in daycare centers. Yet cases of daycare abuse, because they're so news-worthy and because they resonate with parents fears, will always be covered. I would suggest that an inquiring reporter might note, quite apart from the infrequency of daycare abuse, that those cases reveal something very important about a poorly monitored and poorly sup-ported system of daycare for children.

Of course good reporters have done precisely that. All too often, how-ever, this larger context and its attending issues are ignored. I know that these long-term systemic stories about the decline of the infrastructure, about the quality of child daycare, require that a reporter be assigned to a story for a long period of time. These stories are costly, and some editors and reporters will be honest enough—even though I think they're wrong—to say that covering them in this way is the responsibility of social science. I disagree. If the sensational has a place in news coverage, it has it only to the extent that the *context* of the sensational does too.

Third, as you report an unusual incident, report also the most reasonable, reliable evidence of how unusual it is. Have at least some acquaintance with the most recent statistics about how relatively frequent or infrequent the incident you're reporting is. Of course you have to report the abduction of children by strangers. I want to read about each and every one of those cases. I think most people do. But give some sense of just how rare these abductions are.

A fourth and related point is to take great care in reporting crime statistics. Overwhelmingly, press reports of crime are based on the FBI's Uniform Crime Reports, which offer data in a series of categories—homicide, robbery, rape, assault, burglary, larceny, vehicle theft—and that's all. So when newspapers and television stations report crime statistics, they only include these crimes. The UCR keep no statistics for white-collar crime, official corruption, environmental crimes, for example, and that makes them a problematic tool for public education. A compounding problem is that they include only crimes reported to local police departments. By definition they cannot include unreported crimes.

Given these shortcomings, the Uniform Crime Reports are a serious factor in sloppy news reporting. Simple errors can have enormous impact. Consider, for example, per-capita information about crime. Does New York have more murders than any other city? In terms of absolute numbers, yes; but I think the more significant figure is the likelihood of one's being victimized in a given city, and per-capita information is very important to making that calculation.

Reporters can use other crime statistics, from the Justice Department's National Crime Survey, which uses survey interviews to measure crimes *not* reported to the police as well as those that are. Because of the way they're gathered, the Justice Department's figures are considered quite reliable, though only recently has the press begun to pay attention to them. The NCS data provide a much better picture of crime, especially when they are reported alongside the Uniform Crime Reports.

Fifth, if you're going to cover a sensational incident that starts the criminal justice system rolling, follow the case to its conclusion. Don't ignore the rape or the homicide that galvanizes a city, but tell us what ultimately happens to the person who is accused. Let people know that the criminal justice system can take an incredibly long time to adjudicate such an incident. This does happen in the most notorious, high-profile cases, but I think that sometimes gives people a sense that *only* high-profile cases are satisfactorily adjudicated. A lot of less notorious cases seem to drop off the face of the earth. Cover stories to their conclusion, and certainly cover exonerations when they occur.

I once followed a story here in New York of a young man accused of child abuse in a daycare center. I interviewed all the reporters about the story months later and was struck by the fact that three days after the story broke, when the accused was completely exonerated, the papers didn't run a story reporting that fact. Had it been a big high-profile case, it would have merited a big story. But a lot of the middle-range cases just disappear from the news.

Sixth, consider stories about issues that have disappeared and ask why they have. The *New York Times* did just that, I think, in a recent story about how, while homelessness is growing as a problem, it has been in serious decline as a social issue and media topic. Think again of the 1980s explosion of press coverage of child abuse in daycare centers. There's no coverage of that now. Is it because children aren't abused anymore? Obviously not.

One last suggestion. There is a distinguished and truly educative alternative that can complement coverage of the sensational, and that is a story or series of stories that analyze a newspaper's or a television station's performance. Such examinations are extremely rare, but when they're done, as the *Los Angeles Times* did recently, they make a valuable addition to the standard unusual and sensational fare.

These stories are rare, of course, because it takes a lot of guts to let loose an investigative reporter, one of the best, like David Shaw, on one's own newspaper or television station. Shaw won a Pulitzer Prize for his unprecedented four-part series in the *Los Angeles Times,* for which the paper's editors allowed him a lengthy period of time to examine the *Times'* own coverage of the McMartin child sexual abuse case. Shaw looked back at the coverage and concluded that it was flawed by an early, excessive reliance on the prosecution's version of events. He also looked at local television news coverage of the case, and the larger news environment in which the incident was portrayed.

How often can we expect any newspaper or television station to do something like this? Not very often. But can we honestly say that such unflinching self-examinations are not news?

I believe that the unusual and the sensational are valid news, but they become much more valuable when supplemented by news analysis that provides some context to the unusual and the sensational. Let's not deny the role that fear plays in our lives. Let's look it squarely in the face, and try to make some sense of it.

Steven Gorelick is special assistant to the president at the Graduate School and University Center at the City University of New York, and is an adjunct lecturer in the department of communications at Hunter College.

3

The Reporter I:
Cops, Killers and Crispy Critters

David Simon

At the moment you begin reading this, some poor bastard three years out of journalism school is sitting at a video-display terminal in a newspaper office somewhere in these United States, fingers darting on a keyboard. No doubt a cursor flashes through line after line of the same simple, tired equation:

"A 17-year-old West Baltimore youth was shot to death yesterday in a murder that police say is related to drugs...."

Or, perhaps: "The battered body of a 25-year-old Queens resident was found by police along the shoulder of a Long Island expressway...."

Or: "A 43-year-old East Los Angeles man was found stabbed to death in the trunk of his car...."

Behold the entrails of any large American newspaper's metro section—misdemeanor homicides, casualties that will for the most part be interred in four paragraphs or less in those around-the-region packages. Oh sure, if someone is unfortunate enough to be killed in the right zip code, if the victim happens to be famous, if he or she is killed for some unusual motive or in some unusual way ("Police said it was the first slaying involving a staple gun in more than a decade."), then chances are a good newspaper will give it some space. But most violence, when it first crosses a city editor's path, looks decidedly similar: drug murder, drug murder, robbery murder, domestic, drug murder.

As a result much of a city's pain is recorded in that tried-and-true four-paragraph formula, then used as filler on page D17.

A police reporter at the *Baltimore Sun* since 1983, I've probably written a thousand of those briefs, the greater share of them for young black males, killed over drugs or women or disrespect in the parts of Baltimore that don't show up in newspaper market surveys. On my first shift as a police reporter, I went to the night editor with two separate shootings in the 800 block of West Baltimore's George Street, thinking it remarkable that two human beings could be victims of gunfire on a single night in a single block.

"That's the Murphy Homes," the editor explained, allocating two paragraphs for each murder. "When you don't have a shooting there, it's news."

The logic is, of course, inescapable. Every last one of us accepts the dog-bites-man, man-bites-dog postulate as a working gospel. Inner-city violence, the urban drug trade, the devaluation of black and Hispanic life in our cities—all of it has become so common and so certain that we can no longer regard it as unusual. The limited coverage that results is universal, bloodless and devoid of even the slightest suggestion of human emotion:

"A 24-year-old South Philadelphia man was gunned down...."

It's bad journalism. In fact, it's the very essence of what journalism should not be: writing and reporting that anesthetizes readers, that cleans and simplifies the violence and cruelty of a dirty, complex world, that time and again manages to reduce life-size tragedies to easily digestible pieces.

After four years of writing such stuff, I decided to take a shot at something different, something that might break through the sedimentary layers of daily journalism and unearth what I suspected still existed: a world of crime and violence and pain that even the most jaded readers could be made to feel. In 1988, I took a year's leave of absence from my newspaper to join the Baltimore Police Department's homicide unit as an unpaid observer. Through an agreement arranged with the police commissioner and the department's legal affairs unit, I followed a shift of 18 homicide detectives and detective sergeants from crime scenes to interrogations, from autopsies to court trials.

To tell the story of a year in the life of a big-city homicide unit, I did something journalists seldom do anymore—with crime stories or any other fare. I made a conscious decision to write the narrative from the point of view of the central characters: four detectives, two sergeants and a lieutenant in command of the shift. As a result, the reader travels through a homicide detective's daily routine accompanied by a narrator who is, in effect, the communal voice of the homicide unit rather than an overtly detached reporter. That communal voice—like detectives everywhere—was tired, cynical, a little bitter, but more alive and interested in the reality at hand than a reporter's voice ever could be. Example:

"Assuming that the uniforms, upon arriving at the scene, were sharp enough to grab anyone within sight and send them downtown, you then go back to your office and throw as much street-corner psychology as you can at the people who found the body. You do the same thing with a few others who knew the victim, who rented a room to the victim, who employed the victim, who fucked, fought or fired drugs with the victim. Are they lying? Of course they're lying. Everyone lies. Are they lying more than they ordinarily would? Probably. Why are they lying? Do their half-truths conform to what you know from the crime scene or is it complete and unequivocal bullshit? Who should you yell at first? Who should you scream at loudest? Who gets threatened with an accessory-to-murder charge? Who gets the speech about leaving the interrogation room as either a witness or a suspect? Who gets offered the excuse—The Out—the suggestion that this poor bastard needed to be murdered, that anyone in their circumstance would have murdered him, that they only killed the bastard because he provoked them, that they didn't mean it and the gun went off accidentally, that they only fired in self-defense?"

True, this is hardly the restrained, analytical tone of professional journalism. Nor for that matter is it the communal voice of crime victims or witnesses or suspects or defense attorneys—though I would point out that nothing here suggests that books of narrative nonfiction devoted to those perspectives shouldn't exist. Still, the perspective employed here is nothing more or less than the mentality of an American homicide detective, which happens to be the subject matter of my book. Readers seem to understand and accept its stance; so, too, do many other writers of nonfiction and literature alike.

Some veteran journalists, however, read the book and went out of their gourd. They cited incidents in the book in which detectives were revealed as racist or sexist or homophobic or, worst of all, intent on viewing other people's pain as a source of comedy and amusement. Then they railed at a journalist who presented such scenes, dialogue and attitude without distancing himself, without suggesting to readers that these things were wrong or cruel or deserving of criticism.

"Detectives tell the world's best war stories," wrote Edna Buchanan, the *Miami Herald*'s Pulitzer Prize-winning police reporter in her review of the book. "These are men so intriguing, their mission so vital, that a reporter must use caution. You must not be caught up in their charisma and their thinking, you must not become one of them. To a great extent, that is what we witness here, the metamorphosis of the author from reporter to policeman."

I should say here that I like and admire Edna Buchanan (love and admire, before the review), who has done about as much with the daily newspaper medium as any police reporter working today. Neither are these the rumblings of a wounded author; Buchanan's notice was kind at other points and, nationally, reviews of the book have generally been quite favorable. I cite her comments here only because I think they're indicative of a cautious logic that has held sway in newspaper offices for far too long. And to bolster this argument, I'm inclined to drop a name or two.

Damon Runyon, for starters.

Or Frank Ward O'Malley.

Or, better still, Herbert Bayard Swope.

These people, I would suggest, are the lost legacy of American crime reporting, a grand and noble tradition of ambulance chasing that has been squandered in the modern crusade for our feigned, practiced objectivity. Tell the truth: Was there ever a better courtroom tale than that of Damon Runyon's wandering, comic rendition of the sensational Ruth Snyder-Judd Gray trial? Has anyone ever given a better account of police corruption run amok than Swope in his investigation of the Rosenthal murder of 1912? And who can forget Frank O'Malley's *New York Sun* rendering of the murder of Policeman Gene Sheehan, an account told entirely through the words and feelings of the dead cop's mother?

Who can forget it? Practically everyone. Runyon, O'Malley, Swope—these men are no longer influences on American journalism. They exist in newsrooms today, if at all, as apocryphal images of old-time hacks, amusing to us in their innocence. The Rosenthal murder and the ensuing execution of Police Lieutenant Becker? No one remembers anything about it. Long Island's sensational Ruth Snyder case? What exactly was that about?

It's a shame that so few remember—not the crimes necessarily, but the free-spirited ways in which crime reporters used to tell a good story.

Because from generation to generation, violent crime has been one of the great universals in journalism, a daily source of evocative, emotional drama. And if we believe our own publicity, then journalists are supposed to be the great storytellers of every age. Historians will produce the more exacting versions long after anyone ceases to care, while novelists waste their words on make-believe. Reporters, we like to tell ourselves, are there every day to tell the tale first.

And yet as storytellers, we have abdicated.

Every time a reporter sits down and recounts an act of violence in the same time-honored formula—lead, nut graph, best quote, and so forth—something almost as dehumanizing as the crime itself has occurred. Having lost his art, the storyteller is reduced to the mere transmission of facts, and the cost to the reporter, to the news report and to society itself is certain. Repeatedly bludgeoned with crime and violence by every medium, our culture is now so bored with ordinary tragedy that we only become excited by those crimes that are larger, more unlikely and more bizarre.

During the year I spent in the Baltimore homicide unit, the only murders to make the *Baltimore Sun*'s front page involved two separate incidents of arson that claimed the lives of three and two young toddlers, respectively. The rape and murder of an 11-year-old girl, abducted as she walked home from a city library branch, made the front of the metro section. The death of an 81-year-old woman, sodomized and then suffocated in her South Baltimore home, ran on an inside page, next to the weather chart. These are not the results of bad editing decisions, but rather of routine ones—of a process that generates not compelling stories of real people caught in real tragedy, but news articles of compressed, objective fact.

As for the rest of the 234 murders that Baltimore recorded in 1988, they were scattered through the metro section, most of them published as briefs in the regional wrap-up. The inside pages were filled with the drug murders, the domestics, the daily bloodletting of the city's damned in their battered high rises and rotting row houses. In life they meant little to us; in death, even less—interesting to editors and reporters only in their numbers, in the rate and frequency of their deaths or the occasional case in which an odd, unusual fact is noticed.

But what does that say about my newspaper's coverage of the violence that plagues its city? And what does it say about the willingness of reporters and editors to bring the true nature of crime and violence to readers? After all, the burned children, the 11-year-old girl and the 81-year-old woman are the rare exceptions; so, too, are rapes and robberies, which accounted for only 16 percent of Baltimore's murders in 1988. Young black men and young Hispanic men are the real casualties in America's cities, just as narcotics is the real crime of the ghetto.

And worse than the crime that isn't covered by most newspapers is what does get space. Consider the stale, hackneyed form of The Solved Whodunit story, which invariably features two earnest, God-fearing detectives avenging the slaying of a true innocent because they believe in the sanctity of human life. The more honest image of big-city police work is a detective with the files for six drug murders open on his desk, chewing on half a cheese steak and cracking jokes as he looks over the latest batch of morgue photos.

How then, do we write honestly about crime and violence, when crime and violence are so remarkably ordinary? How do we make readers feel routine tragedy? And if we can't ever do that much, how will we make readers see and hear and feel the truth about what's happening in American cities?

More than any other factor, the structure and requirements of modern news organizations encourage ordinary, repetitive crime coverage. After all, the first demand of most newspapers and television stations is that a crime story be immediate, that it follow by hours or a day at most the actual event. Given that simple truth, most crime stories are stillborn. They exist not as long, evocative tales that bring victims and victimizers to life, but as half-finished accounts of facts that can be called certain in the immediate wake of the incident. And in the earlier hours of a murder or robbery or rape, one incident looks much the same as another. It's only in the days or weeks of investigation that follow that the real story begins to emerge; by then the reporters are chasing fresh stories.

Alas, it takes a bold editor to pick one inner-city rape or one drug murder and run with it, telling his reporters to pursue every detail on a story that seems utterly routine. More still, it takes a clever reporter to write his piece as a genuine tale, to bring the human element into a crime story, to see the event as something more than filler for half a news column.

Nothing here argues for sensationalism—for the screaming tabloid journalism in which crime reporters badger witnesses as they race from a courthouse door, or steal graduation photos from the living rooms of grieving mothers. In fact, narrative journalism—properly performed—requires a continuing, cooperative dialogue between a reporter and his news sources. How else can a reporter hope to collect the wealth of detail and insight necessary to tell a story from another person's perspective?

The real ethical threat from the narrative form is hardly sensationalism, but rather the possibility that some reporters will grossly manipulate their sources, as Janet Malcolm suggested in her notable essay, or that some reporters will themselves be manipulated. And yet anyone with sense has to admit that these risks are inherent no matter what style of journalism a reporter attempts to practice.

That narrative tales so rarely appear in newsprint is in part attributable to the fact that the police beat is regarded by most newspapers and television stations as a training ground for young or inexperienced reporters. A year out of journalism schools, the freshman class is taught accuracy and objectivity and a straight news or news-feature style of writing. By the time they're in a position to do anything particularly creative with their subject matter, those who began their careers covering cops have been elevated to more dignified beats.

But in larger part, the decline of great crime reporting is our industry's fixation on objective analysis, our unyielding belief that the stories of crime and violence in our society are best told from a reporter's point of view. True, not every story lends itself to narrative form, and not every tale can be easily told from a character's unique perspective. Nothing reads worse than narrative written by a reporter who doesn't have the background, or the talent, or enough knowledge of his subjects. But when the magic works, it works wonders. To put a reader in the shoes of a defense attorney, a judge, a jail guard, police informant, a killer— that's the glory of storytelling as Runyon and Swope knew it.

Consider Frank O'Malley's wondrous account of a cop killing, published more than 80 years ago:

"You know how he was killed, of course—now let me talk about it, children, if I want to. I promised you, didn't I, that I wouldn't cry anymore," declares the narrator, who happens to be the dead officer's mother. "The policemen all stopped talking when I came in, and then one of them told me it was against the rules to show me Gene at that time. But I knew the policeman only thought I'd break down, but I promised him I wouldn't carry on, and he took me into a room to let me see Gene. It was Gene."

Or the beginning of Swope's classic story of police corruption and murder, told from street-corner level in the New York *World* of 1912:

"Herman Rosenthal has squealed again.

"Through the pallid underworld the sibilant whisper ran. It was heard in East Side dens; it rang in the opium houses in Chinatown; it crept up to the semipretentious stuss and crap games of the Fourteenth Street region, and it reached into the more select circles of uptown gambling where business is always good and graft is always high. Rosenthal had squealed once too often."

Great stuff—literature, of a kind—but does anyone believe that it would get published today? Runyon, O'Malley, Swope— it's not unreasonable to imagine these legends bringing in their best and most dramatic work, only to have the blood drained from it by the clinicians of this enlightened age. To look at what passes for crime reporting in the 1990s is to conclude that objectivity makes cowards of us all.

That's why some of the reaction to my book fascinated me. It's as if journalists so value the weight of our dispassionate voice that we're terrified of allowing any other view—even that of the story's subjects— to dominate. Ms. Buchanan, again: "Homicide cops who daily face a job like no other must grow calluses on their hearts to survive. Without the black humor that makes them laugh, they would surely cry.... But we journalists have no excuse for similar behavior.... It troubles me when Simon refers to a man who burned to death as 'a crispy critter.' Sure, cops talk like that all the time, but not us."

Exactly the point. And when I stood in that fire-gutted row house looking at an arson victim, I had two choices: I could write a book showing readers what it feels like to be a news reporter witnessing a police detective witnessing a tragic death. Or I could get out of the way and write a book from the detective's point of view, granting readers uninhibited access to those who truly labor amid the violence. To David Simon, the dead man in that row house was a horrible sight, something to lose sleep over. But to Richard Garvey, the veteran detective standing next to me, he was a crispy critter. My uneducated guess is that more readers wanted to know what Garvey felt.

To those who defend objectivity at all costs, the implication is that a valuable, essential perspective has been lost when readers are denied the views of David Simon, journalist. But isn't the opposite true? Isn't it more likely that a more precious perspective is gained when a reporter understands his subjects enough to tell a story from their point of view? Logic suggests that if we are ever going to return that lost sense of tragedy and even reality to newspaper pages, we are going to do it not by writing news accounts, but by telling stories. And the best stories are not those in which real people are simply named and quoted and analyzed by some omniscient scribbler, but those in which real people think and act and feel.

In that sense, narrative journalism can in no way be confused with the "new journalism" of an earlier era—a style of writing in which the thoughts and philosophies, visions and verbiage of the writer became as important to the story as the objective reality. Narrative journalism is quite the opposite: It requires a good writer's style and hyperbole to be sure, but at the same time it argues against the writer's unencumbered vision. It is, instead, the vision of those living the reality of the event.

Get it straight: To write that a murder occurred in West Baltimore last night and then list the known details accomplishes nothing. But to visit the scene of that murder from a detective's eye view makes a reader actually feel something. Just as a reader can be made to feel the tragedy through the eyes of the victim's mother, or brother, or girlfriend, who learns of the death at the doors of the emergency room. Even the cynicism of a precinct turnkey, who locks the murder suspect into a holding cell with 20 other souls, tells us more truth than the simple facts of the case.

Critics of such narrative journalism might ask if the journalist's role in the process hasn't been utterly devalued, or if the journalism itself isn't undermined. After all, if a story is best told from a character's point of view, then who is to save readers from being misled by that character's subjectivity?

To that argument I would respond that a journalist who gives himself over to the narrative form does not abdicate his essential responsibilities. Decisions about what information to include and what to leave out, about which quotes should be emphasized or which actions will be recounted— all of that is still within a reporter's bailiwick. Writing in narrative, a reporter doesn't establish his own credibility by denying his characters their subjective viewpoints; he does so by portraying those characters as accurately and as fairly as possible. After that, it's up to the reader.

Example: When I reported and wrote *Homicide* I was fully aware that my detectives were, at moments, racist and sexist and homophobic. And I was also conscious of the fact that their squad-room humor was often little better than cruel banter. I very purposefully kept those moments in the manuscript, left them in every chapter as guideposts for readers seeking an honest view of inner-city cops. True, these ugly moments were revealed to readers from a detective's point of view, but they were revealed nonetheless. And this is the real question: Do readers really need a journalist to stand up and declare that a subject's particular action or statement is sexist or racist or unfunny? Why and to what possible purpose? Such things are usually self-evident, and if they're not self-evident, isn't it better to allow readers a chance to reach their own conclusions? For journalists, the real test of integrity isn't whether you convict or acquit the subjects of your stories, but simply whether or not you present the reader with all the evidence.

Two years ago, I managed to get a long story in the *Baltimore Sun* that told of a drug slaying, and a routine drug slaying at that. I'm particularly proud of the article because it's written entirely from the point of view of the killer, one Donnie Andrews, whom I interviewed from a federal prison over the course of several weeks.

It begins:

Reggie saw him first.

Zack Roach. Hanging with a couple of others on Gold Street stoop, watching touts and runners working a package in the breaking dawn. It was coming on six, but the shop was still open for business. Straight time means nothing at Gold and Etting.

"There he is. There's Zack, there," said Reggie, slowing the car.

"That ain't him."

"Say what?"

"That ain't him," Donnie said again, playing it off.

Reggie cursed. "That's him there. The boy standing up."
It was Zack, all right. On the street. In the open. Donnie looked at Reggie, listened to the tremor in his voice, and knew at that moment that there was nothing else to say, that thing was going to happen.

The murders of Zack Roach and another bystander occur a few paragraphs further into the story, followed by an account of the investigation that eventually led to Andrews' conviction. The killer's history, his view of himself, his drug involvement and his crime are also recounted—but all of it from the gunman's perspective.

True, the article was predicated on a risky premise, and it was hardly the kind of thing that can be called politically correct. Still, the work received a great deal of positive response, both in and out of the news-room; and strangely, no one bothered to suggest that what they had wit-nessed was the metamorphosis of a reporter into a contract killer.

A critic of narrative journalism could rightly point out that Donnie Andrews' view of the crime is hardly objective, that he could well have been shading things to his own advantage. And it could also be said that the views of others involved in the case—prosecutors, police, victims, witnesses—would have been decidedly different. All of that is valid criti-cism: I checked Andrews' account against all of the available police and court records and found no contradictions, but even so it's not unreason-able to assume that he told his tale to his own liking. Nor is it unreason-able to assume that others involved in the murder would give alternate accounts. Those are the risks of narrative journalism; they can be nei-ther denied nor avoided.

But the benefits are equally obvious.

In this rare instance, the city of Baltimore actually sat up and took notice of one drug murder in a thousand. Whatever else they were led to believe, readers were obligated to accept that on a Gold Street corner in 1986, real human lives were involved in a life-size tragedy. Nothing in any of the newspaper's earlier accounts of the crime came close to sug-gesting anything of the sort. Without fail, they began and ended in the same sad place:

"Two men were gunned down early yesterday morning at a West Baltimore intersection known for drug trafficking...."

David Simon, a police reporter with the Baltimore Sun, *is the author of* Homi-cide: A Year on the Killing Streets, *published by Houghton Mifflin.*

II

Views on Crime and Media

4

The Victim: Twice Wounded

Ellen Levin

It was a typically muggy New York City afternoon in late August of 1986 as the station wagon I was riding in made its way down Ninth Avenue to the apartment of my ex-husband, Steve, who lived in Soho. Forty minutes earlier my father had called me at my office and told me that my youngest daughter, Jennifer, was dead.

The car radio was on and I heard a news reporter say, "...the body of the young woman found behind the Metropolitan Museum in Central Park this morning has now been identified as Jennifer Levin...." At the mention of her name, my heart lurched violently inside my chest and I felt a sick, sinking feeling in my stomach. In one split second I fell from a state of denial into shock.

The car finally pulled in front of Steve's building. As if in a slow-motion dream, I was only vaguely aware of the crowds of people gathered about the street. There were uniformed police, cameramen with heavy equipment, news vans, bystanders and curiosity seekers. The driver, a friend, half pushed, half pulled me from the wagon. As I inched my way toward the building's entrance with my friend's help, the police, sensing what was to come, rushed toward me with 15 to 20 reporters and camera technicians at their heels.

I heard the crowd cry out, "It's the MOTHER! That's Jennifer's MOTHER!!" and suddenly I was swallowed up in a near riot, the police pushing reporters, reporters yelling questions at me, cameramen snapping pictures. I felt claustrophobic, unable to breathe, but I turned to the mob in disbelief and screamed, "My God, what's wrong with you people! MY DAUGHTER IS DEAD!"

It was several hours before I knew Jennifer was murdered. The public knew before I did. I overheard my mother's anguished cry, "She was strangled, our baby was strangled." At that moment of horrid truth the phone rang constantly; the intercom buzzed non-stop. Hungry media were looking for comments or interviews, and their zeal, when added to the police investigation going on inside, caused our family even more emotional distress. When Robert Chambers confessed to killing Jennifer later that same evening, the calls increased, the buzzer rang throughout the night and the media set up camp.

This was how I met the press, my introduction to becoming, very much against my will, a "public figure." Since then I have become very knowledgeable about the media, from both personal experience and an insatiable desire to study and make sense of a concept of "news" that pits the press against innocent victims of crime. At issue is the public's right to know versus the victims' right to privacy: where do we draw the line?

Certainly in my family's case, as Chambers' confession was made public and in the ensuing two years until his conviction, if there was an ethical line the media were supposed to observe they crossed it so often as to obliterate it. From the moment the confessed killer was led from the Central Park precinct, the media began a flurry of lurid headlines and journalistic excess, blaming Jennifer for being an architect in her own misfortune. Days after her murder, the New York *Daily News* ran the front-page headline: "Girl's slaying suspect: SEX PLAY 'GOT ROUGH.'" The same day the *New York Post* led with: "Accused killer weeps at video confession, 'I DIDN'T MEAN TO HURT HER.'" The *Daily News* followed the next day with the front-page exclusive: "HOW JENNIFER COURTED DEATH."

This was just the beginning. When the Chambers' family hired Jack Litman to defend their son, things got really nasty. At the time Litman was most famous for his defense of Richard Herrin, a Yale student who was accused of murdering his college sweetheart, Bonnie Garland, in 1977. Herrin smashed her head with a hammer till, in his words, "It split like a watermelon." Litman argued that Herrin was "under extreme emotional distress" as a result of Garland's having broken up with him, and he managed to so successfully implicate Garland in her own death that Herrin was found guilty of manslaughter, not murder. Later, speaking to Dr. Willard Gaylin in Gaylin's 1982 book, *The Killing of Bonnie*

Garland: A Question of Justice, Litman said of Garland, "It was important to taint her a little bit."

To successfully defend Robert Chambers it was important for Litman
to taint Jennifer as well, and Chambers' taped confession was custom-
made for the job. It contained questionable accounts of "rough sex,"
Jennifer's aggressive behavior toward him, and a claim she tried to rape
him. Chambers changed his story three times, but his final version of
events—that he was only protecting himself against Jen—opened the
door for the defense to question my daughter's morality and her behavior, past and present, up to the point of her death.

It also opened the door for the press, for which such a strategy is
perfectly designed for the manufacture of "news." Suggesting reasons
why a particular person was singled out, that the victim was somehow
culpable, makes the public feel fairly safe that this fate could not befall
them. This is what most violent crime news is about, and defense attorneys who can will use the press as a tool to attack the victim and create
doubt about their client's guilt.

Do the media recoil at such gimmickry? Do they ask themselves if
such spoon-fed fare is responsible journalism, or even in the public interest? Some might, but most don't. They know that for whatever pain and
public humiliation a story may cause victims and their families, there is
likely to be a proportionate payoff for them in readers and viewers.

During the first two weeks of the defense and press attacks on my
daughter's reputation, I fell further into despair and grief. One evening I
saw Fox Television's "A Current Affair" re-enact Jennifer's encounter
with Chambers—"from the facts as we know them," according to commentator Maury Povitch. I watched as two actors, one portraying Jen,
the other Robert Chambers, met at a bar. While they talked, she seduc-
tively stroked his back until finally they left the restaurant together. Losing all sense of time, I started screaming at the television set, "DON'T
GO WITH HIM JEN!...DON'T GO INTO THE PARK!!" I ran out to
my terrace on the 29th floor of my apartment building and continued
screaming hysterically into the dark caverns of Manhattan, trying to warn
my daughter of what was to come.

In 1988, when Robert Chambers' trial began, my experience as the
mother of a murdered child attending court every day was made considerably more harrowing by the ever-present hordes of media. After almost two years of dodging the press, changing my phone number to an

unlisted one and refusing to make any comments, my family and I were once again thrown into the public arena and private hell of notoriety. We were besieged by reporters and paparazzi on our way into court, out of court and even on the way to the restrooms, where we sometimes sought a moment of solace away from the courtroom. The bailiffs had more trouble controlling the media than they did the crowds who attended the trial. Except for a handful of sensitive journalists, most gave absolutely no consideration to our situation or our state of mind. As a result of my long ordeal with the media, especially during the courtroom days, I now live with a fear of crowds and crowded places.

I am not alone, of course. Today the media's treatment of victims is a much talked-about subject. Two recent cases in particular have made the public more aware of just how difficult it is for the accuser to face the accused in any search for truth and justice that is moderated, as it were, by the media. First we witnessed the Clarence Thomas nomination hearings, in which Anita Hill, with much courage, made public her version of sexual harassment by Judge Thomas. Most of America, and via CNN much of the world, sat glued to their television sets while Hill recounted the seedy details of private conversations she had had with her employer. Was the truth ever disclosed, or did the unusual publicity make victims of both parties? In the William Kennedy Smith rape trial we were once again electronically plugged into some very personal and sexually explicit testimony. Long before the trial the accuser's name had been made public by such media stalwarts as NBC News and the *New York Times,* and the coverage of the alleged assault and later the trial itself became virtually a national referendum on the accuser's character. In the media's quest to fulfill the public's "right to know," both parties were again further victimized.

For many Americans, the William Kennedy Smith trial was probably the first time they had ever seen a real judicial proceeding, made possible by Florida's permitting cameras in the courtroom. New York State recently experimented with cameras in courtrooms, but when the trial period expired at the end of last year's legislative session the Senate and the Assembly were unable to agree on whether or how to extend the program, and so for now cameras are once again excluded from the state's courts. I'm not sure that's a bad thing. I have been to trials where the camera was turned toward the audience so as to catch the emotional reactions of the parents of a murdered child during grueling testimony.

Although such practices were forbidden in New York's original bill, they have happened and, as far as we know, may happen again. What is the purpose if not for exploitation?

I must also say that opening our courtrooms to the greater public through television is basically an exciting and educational breakthrough. It will give hundreds of thousands of people a firsthand view of our justice system, of how it works and what its shortcomings are. It will introduce, for the first time for many, a true understanding of due process and, unlike Perry Mason, expose the real-life predicaments of both defendants and victims. I believe it will also make for better jurors in the future.

But cameras cannot be allowed to interfere with the quest for justice, and if their presence will inhibit certain witnesses from comfortably testifying or cause unnecessary duress for victims and their families, the presiding judge should either ban them during such testimony or insist on electronic "scrambling" or the "blue dot" to protect the witnesses' privacy. Those media which argue for no restrictions contend that there would be no "show" if they had to secure permission from all the parties, an objection that only confirms my belief that those people who do not object to being filmed are not the entertainment the media are searching for.

Perhaps you think the media are more responsible than that, or in any case less self-serving. Consider, then, the circumstances of the December 1991 unanimous Supreme Court ruling that New York State's "Son of Sam" law was unconstitutional. The law, named for serial killer David Berkowitz (a.k.a., Son of Sam), forbade criminals from profiting from their crimes by offering their story to publishers, Hollywood, journalists or anyone else; and stipulated that any proceeds from such an arrangement be paid to the New York Crime Victims' Board and distributed as restitution to victims and their families. In short, criminals could *tell* their story, but not for money.

The case that prompted Supreme Court review involved a former mobster, Henry Hill, whose story, as told to author Nicholas Pileggi, became the best-selling book *Wise Guy* and, later, the successful motion picture *GoodFellas*. The suit was brought not by Hill, but by Pileggi's publisher, Simon & Schuster, which of course profited handsomely from the book. Why should it sue? *Because Simon & Schuster would never have gotten the book if it couldn't have paid Hill to talk.*

In an interview on National Public Radio's "All Things Considered" the day of the decision, commentator Nina Totenberg asked Pileggi if Hill would have talked without money. Without missing a beat, Pileggi responded, "Not at all." Later in the broadcast Totenberg asked Hill himself, in a phone interview, if he felt it was right for him to profit from his crimes. Hill responded: "Well, I mean, I do a lot of things where I don't get paid today,...but I also have to feed my family. I also have to put my children through school." When Totenberg asked him if he had ever hurt anyone, Hill paused for a moment, then said, "Violence is a part of that life."

So it is. While the Court's decision was based on the *criminal's* First Amendment rights to free speech, the effect is to benefit *media companies* at the price of public safety. It's open season on victims, and I can imagine the publishers, journalists, television and movie producers lining up at the prison gates.

In my case and many others I have been involved with, I have witnessed both good and bad reporting of crime. Our right to free speech under the First Amendment gives the media almost unlimited freedoms, but it is we, the people, who support these rights and therefore can demand they be used responsibly.

Exploiting tragedy and violence, being careless with facts and glamorizing the offender are dangerous abuses that incite communities' hostilities rather than produce a sense of hope and well-being. Our schools of journalism should pay special attention to these defects in our media system, and journalists who cover crime stories should receive some special training in the history and ethical issues of their beat. Editors and publishers should occasionally make decisions based on ethics and responsibility rather than on profits. In the end, with better understanding of victims of crime, will come better, more thorough and professional reporting.

Treating victims of crime with respect, dignity and compassion is a matter of observing their basic human and civil rights. More important, it is a way to help heal, rather than hurt, those who are already wounded.

Ellen Levin lives in New York, where she is a founder of Justice for All, a victims' rights political action committee.

5

The Criminal: Where the Sun Don't Shine

Federal I.D. No. 03144-999

"...in order to enjoy the inestimable benefits that the liberty of the press ensures, it is necessary to submit to the inevitable evils that it creates."
—Alexis de Tocqueville

"HIT THE GROUND! BELLY DOWN, DOWN! MOVE 'N I'LL BLOW YOUR BRAINS OUT. CUFF 'EM, QUICK!"

The man on the ground moans as the man above him recites Miranda in a rapid monotone:

"You have a right to remain silent. If you talk anything you say can and will be used against you in court. You have the right..."

With their hands on the suspects' heads, the cops shove the two men into the squad car and slam the door shut. The prisoners sit caged in the rear. Quietly—the car siren off, its lights on and still spinning—they are taken away.

Two more "bad guys" collared; two more additions to the flotsam and jetsam waiting to be filtered through the slow grinding mess of the criminal justice system.

I wondered, as I watched this arrest from my bedroom window, whether the media would take an interest in these two young black men whose names probably meant little to anyone but their mothers. I imagined that they were about to be swallowed up by a system that is known for producing criminals: more than a million Americans live behind bars; almost one-in-four black 20-something New Yorkers are under court supervision.

Here were two more anonymous citizens about to be reduced further in status; their distinctive street gear replaced by orange jump suits; their names replaced with numbers; their 15 minutes of fame to consist of tallies in a Department of Justice statistical abstract.

There were no hand-held Camcorders rolling that night, no police brutality to witness, no drama to rile the public. The men in the back of the squad car were not the sons of the famous or the infamous.

The public, and hence the media, is not interested in an ordinary arrest. No man-bites-dog story here. The power of the press would neither help nor hurt the two men I saw taken away that night.

As I witnessed the sights and sounds of that arrest—cops barking orders, suspects groaning, cuffs clicking, guns pulled and pointed, red and amber strobes spinning, and constitutionally required warnings cited—I shivered nervously. Several days before, 500 miles away, a drug kingpin I had worked with had been busted by the Drug Enforcement Agency and taken to the Miami Metropolitan Correctional Center.

Edward Christian was a marijuana smuggler, and I was his assistant. He was in jail, and I was near panic that I might be next. Watching the scene outside my window dissolved any calm I had been able to maintain since Eddie's arrest. I imagined the scene I had just observed being replayed, this time with me in cuffs, my wife crying, my children screaming, the neighbors peeking out their windows, and the shame that would follow.

I live in a small suburban village where a broken lock on a merchant's door still draws notice in the weekly tabloid's police blotter page. My arrest would be headline news: CIVIC LEADER CUFFED—Father of Three Arrested—Drug Smuggling Alleged. The words criminal and outlaw haunted my thoughts. I was convinced that the media would jump on me.

Just hearing the hurried words of the Miranda warning outside my window that night had me imagining the taunts my children would be exposed to by their classmates:

"Hey, your daddy's a low-life drug dealer," and "Ha, Ha, your dad's in jail. Didja get some mail from dad in jail?"

My mind's eye was clouded by pictures of my kids coming home to a house in emotional turmoil because daddy was locked up. I couldn't let what I had just witnessed happen to me, at least not in my own neighborhood.

I knew that the DEA and U.S. Attorney were persistent and powerful. Besides, there were too many people involved and too many opportunities for others to talk. I would be named and I would be indicted, but I didn't want to become a media event. For the sake of my family, and for the sake of my personal dignity, I didn't want my life sliced up in order to feed the public lust for personal tragedy.

Scared, I called my lawyer and then my travel agent. I flew to Switzerland the next day to visit my money. I planned to return, but I needed some time to think. I needed some time to map out a strategy in a place that I thought was out of harm's way, a place where I thought I could avoid arrest—at least temporarily. I decided to withdraw some money for my defense and then return home to my family.

Unfortunately, I moved too slowly. Two days later, as I was coming out of Credit Suisse, I was tapped on the shoulder by the Zurich Polizei. No Miranda warning, but also no handcuffs, no lying face down on a black top road, gun to my head with a cop screaming threats to blow my brains out. My arrest was civilized. A simple request to accompany the arresting officer to headquarters.

The Swiss media knew only my first name and my nationality. Swiss law prohibits the publication of a defendant's full name. Only upon conviction does an offender get to see his or her name in print. Even after the trial the judge may seal the case and protect the identity of everyone involved.

Eight months later I was extradited back to the United States. I was brought back to be arraigned in South Carolina. I knew that it would be big news in Charleston, and I hoped it wouldn't reach the media in the Philadelphia suburb where my family lived. When I got off the plane, the local Eyewitness News team was there, but the United States Marshals hurried me into a waiting van and shielded me from reporters. There were pictures, but little publicity.

I was guilty. To avoid a chancy trial, a long sentence and media interest, I pled out. I decided to do my time as unobtrusively as possible. I figured if I quietly paid my debt, and prayed that public notice would be buried in the media's back pages, I could escape notoriety.

Press coverage would have only exacerbated an impossible situation; it could only harm me, my family and our futures. Luckily for all of us, the media gods were merciful, and I didn't become a newsworthy item of gossip.

Leona Helmsley and Michael Milken were not so lucky. Newspaper publishers and TV news directors salivated whenever they had a tidbit to report about the '80s most well-known defendants.

"The Queen of Mean," and "It Rhymes with Rich," were both used to describe Leona Helmsley. In the court of public opinion she was convicted the day she was indicted. The splashy headlines, the puns on her advertising—"The Only Hotel Where The Queen Stands Guard"—and her abrasive personality all worked to doom her from the start. Headline writers and rewrite editors were blessed time and again with a range of verbal and visual images with which to feed a voracious public. In what must count as one of the best presents the media have ever received from a witness, and possibly one of the most quoted statements of the decade, a former employee of the Helmsleys testified that Leona had said: "We don't pay taxes. Only the little people pay taxes."

The picture that most people drew from these words may not have resulted in her conviction, but it couldn't have helped her case either. Although one juror after the trial claimed that "Leona's personality didn't enter into the jury's deliberations," no one outside the jury room believes that it didn't affect the outcome of the trial. No one who followed the case believes that the tabloid euphoria that followed the verdict did nothing to influence the sentencing judge.

The *New York Post*'s front page screeched "Guilty, Guilty, Guilty" in bold red letters—a total of 43 times, 10 more guilty counts than the jury had delivered. *Newsweek* led with "Ding Dong the Witch is Dead" and titled another article "Mean Queen Dethroned." *Time* magazine tapped into public sentiment with its "Revenge of the Little People" headline. Leona became a lightning rod for all that the working man and woman resent about the lifestyle of the "haves." A New York City cabby aptly summed up popular opinion of the hotel queen, "She's the woman I love to hate."

For a great many people Leona Helmsley's trial was a litmus test. They anxiously awaited the outcome of the sentencing to determine whether or not the rich get special treatment. Even in prison, where every big-time trial is discussed *ad nauseum*, and where most often we root for acquittal—or rather against government prosecutors—we gathered around the TV to soak up the latest Leona news. Most guys I spoke to at La Tuna Federal Correctional Institution wanted a conviction and heavy time. "She'll never do time, she's a rich, white bitch. I bet she walks," was a typical comment. Leona Helmsley's holier-than-thou attitude combined with her enormous wealth was resented as much in the joint as in the outside world. Everyone seemed to believe that she would get special treatment because of her status.

She did get special treatment—four years in prison plus community service. Would she have fared so poorly had she been an ordinary businessperson who buys a car, uses it for family outings, and then charges it against the company account? Would she have fared so badly if she had not starred in her own hotel commercials and stayed out of the limelight before the indictment?

Alan Dershowitz, her appeals lawyer, thinks not. He contends, "There's no way she'd get four years in jail if she were a 70-year-old man. The whole problem is Helmsley's manner. If she were a quiet, wifely, subdued woman who stayed in the background she never would have been sentenced to four years, and probably never charged with a crime."

Most of the men—all "legal experts"—who were doing time with me agreed. William, a former judge who's on short-time after serving three years on a bribery charge, told a paralegal seminar I attended at La Tuna that "Leona Helmsley probably could have worked out a deal with the prosecutor, paid the government, and gone home. She's really being punished for her personality, not her crimes."

A stretch of community service is probably the worst an average inoffensive person committing the same crime as the Mean Queen would have had to do. Jail time is usually reserved for people the IRS wants to turn into examples of what can happen if you don't pay your taxes. To borrow and twist F. Scott Fitzgerald a bit: The rich are different, and the obnoxious, publicity-seeking rich are despised. Leona was and still is news. The media eat up the wealthy when they get into trouble. Leona's 15 minutes of fame turned into years of infamy, and it cost her dearly.

Michael Milken did not seek publicity, but he symbolized an era gone bad. Milken was, in the words of people who knew him, "the most private of individuals," but he also personified the "Greed Generation."

From the time the insider-trading scandals began to break, Milken made the wrong public relations moves. As one adviser put it, "Michael made a conscious effort to be rude to the press." David Vise of the *Washington Post* believed that "Michael was really hurt by the decision not to talk to the press until it was too late. It fueled the basic journalistic instinct that if people refuse to talk, they must have something pretty significant to hide. The game was over, the rest was damage control."

Milken's refusal to be media friendly touched off a feeding frenzy that would have put sharks to shame. Milken had offended the Fourth Estate by willfully ignoring its First Amendment prerogatives. When he finally tried to exercise some damage control, it came off clumsy and disingenuous. Ken Lerer, Milken's public relations liaison, concluded that his client was in a no-win situation. He told *Esquire* magazine, "If you told the press Michael was giving a speech, they wrote that he was trying to improve his image, and if you didn't tell them he was speaking, they wrote that he was a crazy recluse."

When Milken took 1,700 inner-city kids to a Mets game at Shea Stadium, media cynics went for the jugular. As one Milken lawyer said, "It was seen as an attempt by Milken to make himself into a hot-dog vendor, a common person. It was a disaster."

It's difficult to claim regular-guy status and whip up public sympathy when you earn $500 million a year—especially when the nation is heading into a recession. It didn't matter that Milken was kind to children and gave millions to charity. In fact, his charity was viewed by many as ostensibly self-serving. His largess was seen as Scrooge running scared, not reformed.

The public perception of Michael Milken was highlighted one afternoon on "The Phil Donahue Show." Sweeping his finger across a group of "Wall Street types," of whom Milken was one, Donahue scoffed: "I mean, you are mostly white, mostly Northeastern, Yale-Harvard types. You are mostly Republican. You were raised in Connecticut. You never ride the subway, so who gives a damn about you guys?" The commoner on the other side of the tube could be heard belching and laughing at these rich men and their predicaments.

The media fed off of Helmsley and Milken. Their problems sold newspapers and airtime as the great unwashed masses tsk tsked and gloated with satisfaction over the poetry of rich people going to jail. Leona's "little people" had gotten their pound of flesh; Milken's billions could not save him—in fact, the money probably did more than the facts of the case to sink him—and Wall Street was chastened. An example had been set and the media could take a large share of the credit—or blame.

The media's double-edged sword came down again, as it often does, on the side of the prosecution. Chris Welles of *Business Week* says,

"Journalists are most often on the side of prosecutors, trashing the high and the mighty. You always look better when you're saying 'Go get those bastards.'"

The story line of the Milken trial was, "Is the government going to get the bad guys?" That's hardly an objective fact-finding position for the media to take, and yet it's easier to sell newspapers when you debase rather than defend the rich and powerful.

For Leona Helmsley and Michael Milken justice turned out to be an issue of bad public relations, not necessarily truth. Going after the omnipotent often takes precedent over fair play when there is a public to satisfy and advertising space to be sold. As H.L. Mencken once observed: "All successful newspapers are ceaselessly querulous and bellicose. They never defend anyone or anything if they can help it...."

When I first started doing time, I listened to the heart-wrenching stories of various cellmates. Few admitted guilt. Most told stories of how they were framed, or threatened into confessing. Typically guys would tell me: "I pled out 'cause the bastards threatened to indict my wife, my grandmother, my brother.... They ain't got shit on me, but I didn't want nobody gettin' hurt. I didn't want my family screwed."

After a while I stopped listening. After a while I realized that if I believed everything everyone was telling me, I would have had to conclude that 98 percent of the prison population was innocent.

The converse is probably closer to the truth. The criminal justice system in the United States is arguably superior to most, but it still makes tragic mistakes. Estimates of wrongful convictions run as high as 10 percent and as low as one-half of 1 percent. The latter figure sounds insignificant until you realize that the annual conviction rate is roughly a million and a half. That works out to about 7,500 innocent people being convicted *every year*. That's a lot of innocent people being deprived of the one condition Americans prize most, freedom.

Fortunately for Lenell Geter, and a few others, some reporters know that there is often a great story lurking in the forgotten precincts of our prisons.

Martin Yant's book *Presumed Guilty* tells the story of Lenell Geter's ordeal. Geter was sentenced to life in prison for a crime he didn't commit. His friends and co-workers were outraged. They took his case to the court of public opinion and finally got him freed—but not until he had spent almost two years behind bars.

Yant writes: "Geter's ordeal began in August 1982, when he was arrested by police investigating a series of armed robberies in several Dallas suburbs. One of those communities was Greenville, where the 24-year-old black engineer worked.

"Geter would be considered an unlikely suspect in most towns. He had recently graduated from South Carolina State College and had a good job with E-Systems, a large military and electronics contractor. He was a religious, nonsmoking teetotaler known for his soft-spokenness and hard work."

Prejudices die hard in a place where until the late 1960s a sign boasting that Greenville had "The Blackest Land—The Whitest People" greeted motorists entering the city. Greenville viewed blacks with suspicion. The populace's attitude towards minorities provided the perfect culture for prosecutorial misconduct and shoddy police work to grow and fester unchallenged.

Lenell Geter was arrested and convicted by an all-white jury presided over by a judge who refused to give Geter's court-appointed attorney time to prepare his case. Consequently, Geter's co-workers, most of them white, were not notified of the trial in time to testify that Geter was at work at the time of the robberies.

Fortunately, through the efforts of Geter's friends, co-workers and the NAACP, his case caught the attention of the local news media. The *Dallas Times Herald* told of Lenell Geter's plight, after which the *New York Times,* ABC News, *People* magazine and Cable News Network all jumped on the story. Finally an award-winning segment on CBS' "60 Minutes" took the prosecution's case apart piece by specious piece. Ten days later a happy and relieved Lenell Geter was released on a bond put up by his friends. Eventually the charges were dropped.

Lenell Geter's experience was at first bitter, then sweet. The media's sword cut decidedly on the side of justice. It helped to free an innocent man, and in doing so it gave credence to the concept of a free press.

Geter is not the only person to be helped by the power of the press. Randall Dale Adams came within three days of being executed for the murder of a police officer. After 12-and-a-half years, he was saved by the efforts of a filmmaker, Errol Morris. Adams' story is immortalized in the award-winning documentary *The Thin Blue Line.*

Joyce Ann Brown, whose only crime was having the same name as a woman who leased the car used in the robbery of a fur store, also benefited from the intervention of "60 Minutes." She served nine years of a life sentence before the media came to her rescue.

Because economics drives the focus of their interest, the media prefer to highlight the rich and famous. Celebrities offer better headlines, more interesting copy, and higher profits. Meanwhile our jails and prisons continue to contain thousands of untold stories of injustice.

The value of a strong independent press to those who are powerless is undeniable. It is an ironic tragedy—one that does our democracy a disservice—that the people who could benefit most by media coverage rarely get it, and often those who attract its attention suffer the ill effects of overexposure.

In my case, I eschewed publicity, and the Helmsleys and Milkens (and Kennedy-Smiths) may at times be crucified by it, but the people who truly need it sit friendless in iron cages throughout the world. Each one deserves at least 15 minutes of the media's time.

03144-999 is the author's inmate number. He now works for The Fortune Society, an organization dedicated to helping ex-offenders.

6

The Cop: Waiting for Good Dope

Kim Wozencraft

*When the tyrant has disposed of foreign enemies
by conquest or treaty, and there is nothing to fear
from them, then he is always stirring up some
war or other, in order that the people may require
a leader.*

—Plato

I woke up early that morning in East Texas, more than a little surprised, as I came to consciousness, that I wasn't suffering from one sort
of hangover or another. Then I remembered that the night before had
been relatively mild. Though we'd bought a few dime bags of some
kind of powder, speed or cocaine, I don't recall which, most of the evening
had been spent smoking hash and listening to music, setting up future
deals. It's a major pastime on the streets, talking that talk about what
kinds of good drugs might be coming down the pike.

The second surprise of the morning came when I reached the living
room and found that there were no stray dealers flaked out on the couch
or floor. Walking the few hundred yards from my apartment to the 7-
Eleven for a cup of coffee and a Sunday paper (how long had it been
since I'd read a newspaper?), I thought in passing about taking an entire
day off, not calling any dealers, not answering the phone when the dealers called me, not answering the door when they came knocking with
their wares. Then again, if I didn't respond I might miss out on some of
those good drugs that might be coming down the pike, not to mention a
new case or two. The bosses were big on results, big on numbers; they

wanted lots of defendants and they didn't particularly care what means we narcs used to get them. Nobody worried too much if one of us occasionally had a "problem," which seemed to be the official euphemism of choice for being strung out, addicted.

I was. My partner was. I didn't know any narcs who weren't.

The paper I read that morning, one of the Dallas dailies, proclaimed that the governor of Texas was declaring "War on Drugs." There would be a blue-ribbon committee. I remember ambivalent feelings toward the hard-line political declarations made by the governor. The small part of me that was still cop (after too long a time undercover) thought, "Finally, a little backup." The part of me that had crossed the line thought, "Who do these assholes think they're kidding?"

That was 1979, when according to the National Institute on Drug Abuse, levels of drug use in the United States began to go down.

By 1982, when Ronald and Nancy Reagan took the War on Drugs nationwide with their "Just Say No" campaign, use of cocaine was peaking, about to begin a decline, and I was running drug-free laps every day in the Big Yard at the Federal Correctional Institution in Lexington, Kentucky. Though a prison sentence isn't the usual goal for narcotics agents on the fast track, I had admitted to cocaine addiction, and I had admitted to perjury. Not that either of those conditions is unusual for street-level narcs, but normally they don't lead to incarceration. Most of the time when agents get seriously strung out they resign and go quietly out the back door, never to be heard from again. Some of them may take up armed robbery to support their drug habits, or perhaps, more accurately, to support their risk/adrenaline/excitement habits, but only if they refuse to leave the department without making some kind of unseemly fuss is prosecution dangled over their heads. That kind of publicity isn't good for The Effort.

I had quit the department shortly after a midnight shotgun attack wounded my partner and me. A couple of years passed before the Feds showed up to ask rhetorical questions about why I'd taken drugs while working undercover.

I spent most of 1982 and a portion of '83 locked up in Lexington. The U.S. homicide rate was on the decline that year. It continued downward until 1984, steadied in 1985, went up in '86 and down in '87. By 1987, Reagan's drug war was in serious political swing, the media had discovered crack (which had actually been around since the late '70s or early

'80s), and the homicide rate began a climb that has yet to slow. Anti-drug/pro-war rhetoric was being flung far and wide, as were DEA agents, who as of 1985 had set up shop in 39 different countries. Not all of the host nations welcomed the agents' presence, but Uncle Sam was able to persuade any less-than-hospitable nations to accept DEA assistance by threatening to take away U.S. aid.

As DEA "advisers" fanned out across the globe, planting American imperialist feet firmly on foreign soil in the name of Reagan's drug war, Attorney General Ed Meese fanned the flames of rhetoric on the home front. At a 1985 meeting of the Washington Press Club, Meese urged journalists to cooperate in the "mobilization of public opinion" against drug use. "Press hard on this story and connect the occasional user with the governments that support this trade." Meese added that reporters should enlighten drug users to the fact that they were "supporting those who are dealing in terror, torture and death." One may presume from statistical reports that no more than 10 or 15 percent of the journalists at the meeting might have been under the influence of assorted controlled substances, and from anecdotal reports that no more than 50 percent of them were under the influence of alcohol, so it is probably safe to say that at least a quarter of those listening to the Attorney General were of sufficient sobriety to understand that when he spoke of dealers in terror, torture and death, he was not referring to Bill Casey or Oliver North.

Spencer Claw, then editor of the *Columbia Journalism Review,* said in reply that it was not Meese's place to "tell reporters to help the government push a particular point of view.... That's exactly the role that's allotted to the press in socialist countries. The function of the press in socialist countries is to educate people and persuade them about the truth as the government sees it."

Mr. Claw's objections aside, one would be hard-pressed to show that the mainstream U.S. media, whether print or electronic, have been doing anything but pushing the government's view, serving it up in style to a public whose appetite for war and violence is unrivaled in the history of the industrialized world.

Didn't America love "Miami Vice"? Well, here it is, live at five, right in your hometown, and those aren't actors there on your TV screen. We're talking real cops, real dealers, real drugs, guns and blood.

And white middle America, those who consume around 70 or 80 percent of the illicit drugs taken in this country, can sit back in their living rooms and watch evening news visuals that 47 percent of the time show black people with drugs, even though African Americans actually consume less than 20 percent of America's illegal substances, whether homegrown or imported. What's shown on television are inner-city ghetto scenes, cops kicking down doors and dragging "them" off to jail. As though *"it's a black thing, man."*

Even though it isn't. Just as opium wasn't necessarily a Chinese thing in the 1890s, cocaine wasn't just a black thing in the 1920s, alcohol wasn't simply a gangster thing in the '30s, LSD wasn't exclusively a hippie thing in the '60s, and marijuana wasn't solely a Mexican thing in the 1970s. One might go so far as to consider a tendency on the part of the U.S. government to further racial persecution under the guise of drug enforcement, and a tendency on the part of the media to buy into the program wholesale.

Which really came first? The drugs? Or was it poverty, lack of education, unemployment? While crack cocaine and heroin addiction are certainly symptomatic of larger, much more serious problems in America's inner-city ghettos, the propensity on the part of politicians and the media has been to focus drug-war hype on those areas. Meanwhile, the inclination of the criminal justice system to focus enforcement efforts on those areas has been far more dangerous and damaging to ghetto inhabitants and to America-at-large than the drugs themselves could ever be.

Drug war demagogues would have America believe that the youth of America are dropping dead in untold numbers as a result of controlled substance use, and the media encourage this perception by choosing, presently, to highlight stories about crack users who run amok. When I was in graduate school in 1986–88, the beginning of prime time for crack hysteria, I resided in a pretty rough neighborhood in New York City. There was a small vestibule on the first floor of the apartment building where I lived, and when winter came around various groups of crackheads would gather there to fire up. I had to pass through the cramped room every day on my way to classes. Even when the smoke was still hanging in the air, the people sitting quietly against the wall were never anything but polite to me, shifting around to give me passage and saying things like, "Sorry," or "Excuse us." They never even asked me for a handout, much less tried to rob me for drug money. Crack did not turn them instantly into the raving lunatics we've all read about in magazines and newspapers.

Before crack it was cocaine; before cocaine it was heroin; before heroin, speed; before speed, LSD; and, way back, it was the Demon Killer Weed, Marijuana. Granted, many drugs are dangerous. But the fact is that in the United States in 1989, there were fewer than 3,000 deaths from abuse of all illegal drugs combined. The selfsame politicians who keep laws on the books that cause around a million people a year to be locked up for various drug offenses continue to vote for subsidization of the tobacco industry, in spite of the fact that, also in 1989, there were nearly 400,000 deaths from cigarette use. And 48,000 from alcohol use and abuse. Headlines proclaim a multibillion dollar drug-war budget as politicians clamor and shout that they are on the bandwagon, fighting the good fight, trying to save yet another generation of young Americans from the scourge of drugs. What we do not hear about is that 70 percent of those funds goes to enforcement, the leftovers to education and treatment. More cops, more courts, more prisons and jails. Forget about the thousands of addicts who are waiting in line for treatment but can't get into what programs there are. Forget about the thousands of completely needless deaths from AIDS spread through contaminated needles. Though the transmission rate of the virus among intravenous drug users is reduced drastically (to as low as 3 percent) in states where new, sterile needles are available over the counter at the local drugstore, most states continue to enforce laws designed to force addicts to use old needles and share them with other users. Forget too, about the violence—the armed robberies, the muggings, the gang wars— that politicians and the press continue to associate with drug use in spite of the fact that the violence is not about drugs at all. The violence is about money. The violence is about profit. And as long as drugs are illegal, the incredible profits will continue to be there. America now incarcerates a higher percentage of its total population than any other country in the world, and incarcerates a higher percentage of black males than does South Africa.

According to the Sentencing Project in Washington, D.C., in 1990, almost one in four black men in the 20-29 age group were either in prison, on parole or on probation; many, if not most, for drug offenses. White males in the same age group averaged one in 16 under justice system control. Looking at the 20/80 percent split for drug use in America, one might conclude that the drug war is being waged almost entirely on minorities, all out of proportion to their actual involvement in drug abuse.

Instead of reasoned debate on the topic, we read, in such esteemed chronicles as the *New York Times:*

"A New Purified Form of Cocaine Causes Alarm as Abuse Increases."

Who's alarmed? It's in the lead: "A new form of cocaine is for sale on the streets of New York, alarming *law-enforcement officials and reha-bilitation experts* [italics mine] because of its tendency to accelerate abuse of the drug, particularly among adolescents." The article goes on to describe DEA seizure of half a pound of cocaine at a crack house. Agents claimed the dealer was "reputedly" producing 2.2 pounds of crack each day, for daily profits of $500,000. There is no mention of how agents arrived at the 2.2 pound figure, no mention of surveillance, infor-mants or any other backup for the "facts." It is simply speculation or manipulation on the part of the DEA, but the reporter bought it. The agents' message was passed on, unchallenged, unquestioned, to the pub-lic. No doubt it succeeded in angering a goodly number of readers who might get miffed at the idea of some miscreant selling death on the rocks and making half a million a day, tax free, by doing so. But by accepting the agents' assertions without looking at what might be behind them, the reporter wrote an article that did little to inform and much to inflame. Just what the agents and experts wanted. The bigger and badder the drug problem is perceived to be, the more job opportunities, grant opportuni-ties, power-seizing opportunities and corruption opportunities there are for politicians, law-enforcement officials and rehabilitation experts.

One very symbiotic method of focusing public attention on drug is-sues is through use of "the celebrity bust." The press gets an instant story; the politicians and enforcement agencies get to show just how insidious and far-reaching drug abuse has become. The civil rights of the celebrity target are of no major concern, at least not until the trial rolls around, by which time the damage has been done. The names Bob Dylan and John DeLorean come to mind. And the name Marion Barry. If "everyone" knew the mayor had a taste for crack and for illicit ro-mances, it didn't take a gang of rocket scientists to figure out that if they could get him into a hotel room with a seemingly willing woman and a crack pipe, they might get some interesting things on tape. Back in the days when Americans had civil rights, this "sting operation" might have been considered entrapment. And the videotape might have been re-served for its purported purpose—as evidence in a criminal trial. No more. When the tape aired on national newscasts, the stark black and white images of DEA agents bursting into the hotel room as the mayor puffed on a crack pipe looked almost as authentic as the crime re-creations (or is it recreations) that have become the mainstay of today's popular tabloid TV journalism programs. Mr. Barry went to jail, but was later in 1994 re-elected mayor of Washington. One wonders why the mayor of the nation's capital wasn't even afforded the same kind of treatment offered to major league athletes when they are discovered to have drug problems.

As though there aren't enough drug stories to go around, reporters lately seem compelled to drag the issue into stories that have absolutely nothing to do with drugs. Reporters covering the Luby's Cafeteria shootings several years ago in Texas felt the need to inform readers that the shooter may have used marijuana sometime in the distant past and chose for the accomplishment of his carnage a semiautomatic that is the current weapon of choice for drug dealers. No drugs were found on the gunman, and there were no indications that he was even slightly intoxicated during his death spree. Yet for some reason reporters felt it necessary to supercharge a story that already had more than sufficient violence in it with references to drug dealers.

A recent "Journal" article in the *New York Times* opens with:

> Dusk settled over a windswept South Bronx street as several teenagers chopped an agricultural product that they will later stash into bags. The next day these same youths would deliver the goods to chic addresses on the East Side and in Greenwich Village, where their customers would rip open the bags, burn their contents and savor the sweet-smelling smoke.

> The bags are not burlap, not glassine, and the chopping is done with axes, not razors.

> "These youths deal in firewood."

The message here seems to be that we should all be astonished to discover teenagers in the Bronx who are *not* dealing drugs. The reasoning may be that if "uplifting" stories don't sell newspapers, perhaps spiking them with a stiff dose of drug-war stereotyping will catch the reader's eye.

One of the things I most regret whenever I look back on my days as an undercover officer and prisoner is that I was ignorant of the role of the press in American society. At a certain point in my final investigation I went to the sergeant and to the chief and tried to stop the thing, told them cases were bad, told them of my own and my partner's drug use. They said take a few days off and then get back out there and make more cases. I knew that if some of the more hard-core speed dealers found out I was a cop there was a very real possibility they might try to kill me. I wasn't sure how the chief would feel if I tried going over his head to the district attorney to explain how the investigation had gotten out of control. But there was the very real possibility that he would feel the same way the speed dealers might if they knew I was a cop—that I was better off dead.

I had never heard the term "Fourth Estate," and so when I found myself strung out on cocaine and stonewalled by the sergeant and chief of police in a town where nobody else even knew I was a cop, it did not occur to me to turn to the local media as a way to fight the authorities.

After we "busted out," rounded up the dealers, talking to reporters very definitely occurred to many of the more than 100 defendants that my partner and I had made cases on. Suddenly, I could not pick up a paper without reading accusations of wrongdoing on our part. Many of the allegations were accurate, some were exaggerated, some were simply lies. A couple of reporters from the Dallas papers latched onto the story and did not let go. I believed they were after the truth, but that didn't ease my feelings of being pursued by a lynch mob.

Now, years later, I look back at that scenario and say, "Bravo." They were doing what they should. Asking questions, digging, hounding, pursuing. They were refusing to swallow whole the lies of the politicians— in this case a chief of police who denied that anything was even slightly out of line in our investigation. After I pleaded guilty before the courts, I spoke to reporters and told them what had happened, this after months of denying accusations. I had hopes that my coming forth might stir up some trouble, might result in some pressure being brought to bear on those who were in charge of the drug war in Texas. I think the reporter did, too.

Though I see evidence that there are still some true investigative reporters trying to dig out the facts from beneath layers of obfuscation, the tendency with drug stories seems to be toward grabbing a quick quote or sound bite, laying out a brief scenario according to some official's version of events, and filing the story. During some of America's more recent "conflicts"—Grenada, Panama, Iraq—the media rightly became outraged when military authorities attempted to control the content of stories by controlling the media's ability to move freely within the area, or, if you prefer, the theater, of conflict (except in the case of Grenada, where they were excluded completely until mop-up time), by requiring the members of the press and electronic media to travel in prearranged "pools," and by carefully controlling all press conferences. Perhaps Panama is a bad example, though, as it wasn't so much a military conflict as it was a military invasion of a country in an attempt to serve an arrest warrant on Manuel Noriega.

The drug war, on the other hand, a war that is being waged in large part against Americans by a select group of politicians and law-enforcement agencies, seems not to merit the aggressive reporting that wars against other nations do. It's there in the semantics of the headlines, it's there in the tone of the articles: drugs are evil; when it comes to banishing them, anything goes, even slipshod journalism.

As the lines between entertainment and news blur into categories with names like "infotainment" and "docudrama," as news broadcasts get slicker, glossier and less substantive, as media specialists show their clients how to give a good press conference, the public gets more of exactly what the politicians and enforcement agencies want them to hear and less accurate, unbiased news.

The same profession that has fought aggressively for the freedom to say what they want when they want about whom they want, provided they can back it up with facts, is shoving drug-war propaganda down America's open throat with a zeal unmatched, except perhaps by that of TV evangelists.

And, to be sure, the same desire for social control that drives the religious zealots who preach via TV drives those who attempt to regulate the average American citizen's constitutionally given right to control his own mind and body.

Representative Charles Rangel, chairman of the House Select Committee on Narcotics Abuse and Control, said in a 1989 *New York Times* op-ed piece that the drug legalization issue belongs "amid idle chit-chat as cocktail glasses knock together at social events." If those same socialites who can so comfortably knock together cocktail glasses (remember, alcohol killed over 48,000 people in 1989) chose instead to pass around a joint or two of marijuana (which has never been documented to cause even a single death), the authorities could not only come in and arrest the guests, they could seize the house in which they were smoking and hang onto it at least until the trials began and perhaps forever. But they probably wouldn't. No self-respecting journalist is going to show up to cover so ordinary a story. The times demand knocking down doors with battering rams and dragging off ghetto inhabitants, half-naked and in handcuffs. *That's* infotainment!

Perhaps if the champions of the First Amendment were more often painting an equitable portrait of the realities of the drug war rather than falling for the sensationalistic stories that are so often orchestrated by law-enforcement agencies, the larger public would begin to question the wisdom of allowing the President, the Congress, the Supreme Court, and their enforcement arms to wage war against the citizens of the United States, and particularly against those disenfranchised members of our society who are least able to defend themselves against the massive, overwhelming power of the United States government.

Kim Wozencraft is author of the novel RUSH, *which MGM released as a motion picture in 1991. While working on her MFA degree at Columbia, she served as a research assistant for the* Media Studies Journal.

7

The Lawyer: "A Chill Wind Blows"

William M. Kunstler

As I enter these observations into my word processor, the trial of William Kennedy Smith for rape, euphemistically characterized by the Florida Criminal Code as sexual battery, is taking place in a tiny courtroom in West Palm Beach. The proceedings, along with comments by selected lawyer experts, are being televised live on CNN and Court TV, with recorded segments later aired on national and local news programs. One network has even gone so far as to assemble what it terms "a shadow jury" to comment on each day's testimony. Newspapers daily devote considerable space to reports of the trial, together with a plethora of opinion pieces. The prosecution of a routine crime, flamboyantly billed by one press source as "the most important trial of the year," is being afforded the full treatment.

From a strict civil liberties viewpoint, it is obvious that given such media coverage it is next to impossible for anything approximating the ideal of a therapeutically fair trial to take place. Each side has taken full advantage of the situation to trumpet its message to the public in general and the jury pool in particular. Virtually all details of the available evidence have been widely disseminated, along with the respective positions of the defense and prosecution camps. Many of the prospective witnesses, some for substantial remuneration, have broadcast their versions of what happened in the wee hours of the morning of March 30, 1991, both at the Au Bar bistro and the Kennedy family estate. In the long run, it might have been far better to have the case decided by telephone call-ins to a tabulating agency rather than in Judge Mary E. Lupo's courtroom.

However, to criticize substantial, even overwhelming, press coverage as an impediment to a fair criminal trial presupposes that, in this society, such trials are possible. Since I firmly believe they are not, the publicity given to Mr. Smith's case becomes relatively meaningless. He has had ample opportunity and resources to use the media to his distinct advantage—to humanize himself, sully his accuser, promote the grainy myth of Camelot and blunt the evidence against him, while the prosecution and some of its witnesses have been more than willing to deal in the same coin.

Unfortunately, in most of the high-profile criminal cases that grace the national landscape, other defendants, excluding well-placed ones accused of white-collar offenses, have not been able to help their causes in the same manner and with the same effect as Mr. Smith. In those instances, the prosecution almost always races from the starting gate with a widely reported and often lavishly staged press conference, referring to the accused as, in one case, "merchants of death," in another as "mindless murderers," and, in a third, as "heinous thugs." Since the objects of these acerbic descriptions are almost always incarcerated on exorbitant bail or none at all, they are hardly as free as Mr. Smith to respond publicly, even if there were any real media interest in their ripostes. Moreover, given their typical lack of financial resources, they cannot hire public relations specialists to allay the dismal portraits painted by their adversaries and have to depend on low-key and often inexperienced court-appointed attorneys for their defense.

The result is that any juries eventually seated in their cases have been thoroughly exposed to at least an initial barrage of devastating pretrial publicity that neither time nor effort can effectively dispel. Whatever may be the sins of General Manuel Noriega, and they may be many, it is impossible to discount the prejudicial broadsides leveled at him, via the press, by the United States government, both before and after his indictment: Tortilla flour in his home portrayed as cocaine and alleged criminal links between him and everyone from Fidel Castro to members of the Medellin drug cartel were but two of the assertions that were liberally leaked to the expectant media long in advance of trial. Although the presiding judge frequently fantasized aloud that an impartial jury could be seated, the utter impossibility of such an accomplishment was readily apparent to anyone who bothered to think about it.

The responsibility for seeking and finding press outlets for defendants with "newsworthy" cases falls squarely on the shoulders of the defense counsel. Whenever and wherever practicable, fire must be met with fire, and it is often only lawyers who have any chance of igniting a flame friendly to their clients. Stimulating the formation of outspoken defense committees; placing advertisements in local journals; holding press conferences and public rallies; writing news releases, letters to the editor and op-ed pieces; and making radio and television appearances are but some of the avenues that may be open to them and their clients. For the usual run of defendants, no matter how titillating the facts of their cases, the struggle for helpful exposure must be waged imaginatively, and even ingeniously, by those lawyers who have their clients' best interests at heart.

But the struggle is a difficult one at best. The courts and the various attorney disciplinary agencies have erected many barriers against this kind of an approach. The Supreme Court has just intimated that defense lawyers may soon be barred from commenting publicly on their criminal cases, while there is a battery of ethical canons designed to curtail what some have labeled "trial by press." The result has been that, after the prosecutor's horse has long since left the barn, the accused may be hard-pressed to close its doors. Most defense attorneys have been reduced to muttering "no comment" to inquiring reporters, and their clients to hiding their faces behind a hat or hand.

Unless the defendant accused of heinous crimes has the money necessary to purchase the services of specialists who can reach and manipulate the press, they are doomed to accept the slings and arrows without an adequate response. Sometimes the presence of a well-known defense attorney can stimulate media interest in a client's side of the story, but in the main, even when counsel is inclined to run the risk of a contempt citation or professional disciplinary action, it is generally impossible to blunt the prosecutor's initial bombast or the media's adverse treatment of the pariahs accused of such offenses. The recent coverage of the New York youths charged with the savage beating of a woman styled as the "Central Park Jogger" is but another classic example of this point.

That case also serves as a graphic reminder that when, in addition to the loathsome nature of the crimes, the defendants are black and the victim white, the media almost always reflect the dominant community's racial attitudes and fears. Feminist Gloria Steinem once authored an op-ed piece in the *New York Times* in which she contended that, in a number of recent incidents, if the races of the protagonists had been reversed, the press and public reaction would have been completely different. Suppose, she wrote, that Bernhard Goetz, the so-called subway vigilante who gunned down four black youths in a New York subway car, were an African-American and his quarry white; could anyone seriously maintain that the community would have widely supported his actions and a jury found him not guilty of attempted murder? Her hypothesis was soundly confirmed when a number of white St. John's University students, accused of plying a black woman with liquor and then sexually abusing her, received the most gentle treatment from the press, and the first three to be tried were acquitted. It is hard to imagine that, had they been black and the woman white, the case would have had the same result.

We exist in a day when the Bill of Rights, about to enter its third century, has been virtually destroyed by a Supreme Court majority determined to reduce it to nothingness insofar as the rights of criminal defendants are concerned. The nullification of federal habeas corpus as a meaningful remedy for unjust convictions; the "good faith" exception to the Fourth Amendment's proscription of unreasonable searches and seizures; the validation of coerced confessions; the reincarnation and extension of the death penalty; the denial of free counsel to indigent capital defendants after the exhaustion of their direct appeals; anonymous juries; preventive detention; the permissible destruction by the police of exculpatory evidence; draconian prison sentences; and penal institutions that would put the Marquis de Sade to shame represent just two handfuls of examples of this insidious process. Even the slight respite provided by the failure of the House and Senate conferees to reconcile their respective chambers' versions of the pending anti-crime bill—which, among other things, creates more than 50 new federal capital offenses—will undoubtedly disappear when the Congress reconvenes in January. Small wonder that Justice Blackmun, in a vigorous dissent in 1990, bemoaned that "a chill wind blows."

With so many of the procedural and substantive safeguards of yesteryear fast disappearing, criminal defense lawyers are left with only their professional abilities and their wits to change the atmosphere surrounding their clients for the better. While many of them fully realize that, as civil libertarian Zechariah Chafee Jr. observed almost a half-century ago, "The press is a sort of wild animal in our midst—restless, gigantic, always seeking new ways to use its strength," they also know that it is the only vehicle by which their clients can hope to offset, even minutely, the state's awesome advantage. In short, they have no alternative but to use it if those for whom they stand responsible are to have the slightest chance to obtain what the frieze over the Supreme Court Building so hypocritically promises to everyone—EQUAL JUSTICE UNDER THE LAW.

More importantly, they must use the press because they know there are few meaningful appellate routes open to them should their clients be convicted. Given the virtual destruction of the Bill of Rights and the presence of so many right-wing ideologues on the federal bench, they must win, if at all, at the trial level. Despite the debilitating inroads the government has made into the jury system—dramatized by anonymous venires and the elimination or sharp restriction of attorney-conducted voir dire—there is still a hope, slim though it may be, of attaining a modicum of justice at this juncture of the criminal process. In this respect, the ability of an accused to attract media attention becomes paramount; and, in my opinion, defense attorneys worth their salt, who are remotely conscious of the mythology of fair trial pretensions, have a solemn obligation to reach out, by any means necessary, to try to equalize the gigantic odds against their beleaguered clients.

In doing so, however, they have to keep in mind the Supreme Court's recent 5-4 decision in *Gentile v. State Bar of Nevada*. While reversing a recommendation that an attorney be privately reprimanded for holding a press conference the day after his high-visibility client's indictment— at which he contended not only that his client was innocent but that the police were guilty—the Court continued to champion the mythology that fair trials in such cases are possible. Moreover, Chief Justice Rehnquist's dissenting opinion in the case, joined by Justices Scalia, White and Souter, must be given new and serious consideration, since Justice Marshall's departure from the Court may well presage a drastic shift in the Court when first it has the opportunity to make it. As Rehnquist put it, "[E]xtrajudicial comments on, or discussion of, evidence which might never be admitted at trial and *ex parte* statements by counsel giving their version of the facts obviously threaten to destroy [the] basic tenet [that impartial jurors must decide cases on the evidence before them in a court proceeding]."

The handwriting on the wall was clearly legible when Rehnquist went on to remind lawyers that they are "key participants in the criminal justice system, and the State may demand some adherence to the precepts of that system in regulating their speech as well as their conduct." The dissenters recognized that comments by defense attorneys have their "maximum impact... when public interest in the case was at its height immediately after [the client] was indicted." Yet by all rational standards that is precisely the moment when it is reasonably possible to neutralize the prosecutor's opinion gambit most effectively.

Even though the majority opinion in *Gentile* seems to indicate that there can be no material prejudice to a fair trial "when the lawyer's publicity is in response to publicity favorable to the other side," Rehnquist brushes this dictum aside by arguing that "the basic premise of our legal system is that lawsuits should be tried in court, not in the media." Naturally he ignores the practice of prosecutors the country over who inaugurate criminal cases by emitting a blast of pretrial publicity wholly detrimental to the defendant. Simply put, Rehnquist does not want to take this arrow from the State's ample quiver or permit those wounded by it to blunt its impact. With the substitution of Clarence Thomas for Marshall, a majority that has shown itself more than willing to depart from established precedent when doing so suits its purpose may soon try to eviscerate the ability of defense attorneys to do what is necessary for their clients.

When that day arrives, we will have entered the wasteland of the criminal justice system and resuscitated latter-day Star Chambers. The State will be free to poison the prospective triers of the fact *ab initio* while those it seeks to destroy will be shorn of even their limited opportunities to preserve their lives or their liberties. The administration of justice will have become nothing short of a grotesque, or, in the words of Franz Kafka, "a summary court in perpetual session."

This is exactly what those in true command, despite their protestations to the contrary, want it to become. The police, the prosecutors, the judges and the wardens are the key social bulwarks against what psychologists and economists so often refer to as the "underclass," and their chief function is to warehouse a significant number of that caste so that their counterparts who wait outside the walls, in bitterness and frustration, will remain relatively quiescent. Police precincts bear such revealing sobriquets as "Fort Apache," and courthouses, "The Fortress."

Prosecutorial misconduct that facilitates convictions, even when uncovered, is never punished.

The concept of due process, once so malleable to the attainment of the ideals expressed in the Fifth and Fourteenth amendments, has now been reduced to such gross pontifications as "criminal defendants are not entitled to perfect trials, only fair ones," as the Supreme Court once put it in denying a new trial to a murder defendant when it was disclosed, long after his conviction, that one of his jurors had applied for employment with the prosecutor as soon as he was seated, a fact that was carefully hidden from the defense until the jury's verdict, and then only revealed quite by accident.

This is the context in which the government seeks to tighten the noose around the necks of defendants by denying them access to the media, and the dilemma that this state of affairs poses for counsel for pariahs of any stripe is a critical one. If they truly believe that their only duty is to their clients, they simply cannot regard themselves, as Rehnquist put it in an earlier dissent, as "an intimate and trusted and essential part of the machinery of justice, an 'officer of the court' in the most compelling sense." This is particularly so for those attorneys who, like myself, believe that "the machinery of justice" more figuratively resembles the Iron Maiden than it does the traditional female figure with the bandaged eyes and the equally balanced scales that adorns so many courthouses throughout the land.

For us, it is impossible to accept the hyperbole of one justice that "the American judicial trial remains one of the purest, most rational forums for the lawful determination of disputes." We must fight our client's battles with every weapon at our disposal, even if such an approach may expose us to the most serious of professional consequences. We are in a war for what author E.L. Doctorow once characterized as "the idea, the virtue, the truth of America," and we cannot yield an inch if we are to remain faithful to our profession and our innermost selves.

William M. Kunstler is a founder, vice president and volunteer staff attorney for the Center for Constitutional Rights in New York.

8

The Judge: Justice in Prime Time

Thomas S. Hodson

As a trial lawyer and former trial judge who was trained as a journalist, I have seen the judicial system from all sides. Frankly, the media's portrayal of criminal justice, and the public's apparent obsession with it, frightens me. When I sat on the bench I always wondered about any reporter I saw in my courtroom. Often I knew that the reporter had no idea what I was doing, what the judicial system was about, what the language being used in the courtroom meant, and what rights were being protected and advanced through the legal system. Rarely do reporters have any expertise in the law; the vast majority come from journalism or liberal arts schools, not law schools. Covering "cops and courts" is usually an entry-level position at newspapers and is subject to general-assignment reporting at television stations. Trained court reporters are a dying breed. Turnover is high.

As a result of this ignorance of the system, the public usually gets superficial and inaccurate reporting on the judicial process. Reporters often portray the judiciary merely as an extension of the prosecutors and police, and commonly overemphasize the day-to-day proceedings of the court without looking at the entirety of the judicial system. Court reporting is therefore often inaccurate, sensational, oversimplified, distorted and routine.

To be fair, many judges and court staffs do not help matters; they do not work well with the news media to ensure accurate reporting. Judges, I have learned, usually don't like reporters, and they certainly do not trust the news media. Many won't talk to the media because they fear their words will not be treated fairly; others ban cameras from their courtrooms because they feel cameras might taint the fairness of the proceedings.

Some of this tension exists because judges, attorneys and journalists view the news media's role in covering the criminal justice system differently. If you took an informal poll, most judges would say that one of the main functions of the press should be to educate the public about the system. Trial attorneys, on the other hand, view the media as something to be manipulated to create an advantage for a client. And the press sees its function as being a public watchdog—to expose abuses and to cover noteworthy cases.

A final, aggravating factor in the relationship between the media and the courts is that those of us in the judicial system find that there are no enforceable rules when working with the press. Courtrooms, by contrast, are governed by rules: rules of evidence, rules of procedure, rules of decorum. No such rules exist in our media relations, and that makes judicial participants in the process extremely uncomfortable.

Truly, the interrelationship between the media and the courts is an adversarial one. Scholars may debate whether it is the public that has the inherent appetite for crime, violence and the drama of the criminal justice system, or whether it is the news and entertainment media that have created the demand. From my perspective the answers really do not matter. What does matter is that the public is being misled by sensationalism and as a result has an abysmally poor knowledge of our judicial system.

And it's getting worse. The term "feeding frenzy" appropriately describes the relationships between the public, the media and the criminal justice system. There is a daily ritual, it seems, in which each group feeds off the other: the news and entertainment media feed large portions of information and misinformation about the criminal justice system to the general public—at the same time feeding off the criminal justice system for raw material—and the system itself is fed and supplied by members of the public, who are not only the consumers of news and entertainment but also, and often unhappily, victims, defendants, witnesses, jurors.

The respective appetites are insatiable. Today people do not want just more general information. They want more detailed information, more lurid stories and more gruesome descriptions. To meet this craving, the media provide such events and package them in competitively attractive formats. The role of the criminal justice system appears to be to create situations the media can use to supply the public's cravings. And, who is the grist for the courts' mill? The members of the public who demand the information in the first place. They become players and stars in the system they yearn to observe.

Public preoccupation with crime is not new. Crime excites and stimulates us. Whenever we hear of a crime, we almost always relate to it personally: "Aren't we lucky that didn't happy to us?" "He'd have to be crazy to have done that." "I wonder if that person is really guilty?" "In what neighborhood did that happen?" "She must have asked for it."

At their best, extrajudicial examinations of crime allow us to look into the dark unknown of our souls. Think, for example, of the great works of literature and drama in which an act of crime becomes, for better or worse, the defining moment for the hero or heroine. But such examinations are rare, and now, in the information age, almost irrelevant in the explosion of media crime and gratuitous violence. In my lifetime, crime has become an increasingly central part of our society's entertainment. Old movies gave us a glimpse of the criminal unknown through gangster characters played by James Cagney and Edward G. Robinson. Old radio shows such as "The Shadow," "Sam Spade" and "Ellery Queen" focused on crime and crime stoppers. The early days of television offered shows like "Dragnet," which filled our non-working hours with suspense and thrills.

But today that kind of fare seems almost quaint. A recent estimate indicated that 60 percent of local television news is devoted to "cops and courts," and that coverage increasingly emphasizes the seamier and more abnormal aspects of the criminal justice system. Courtroom dramas such as "People's Court" and "Divorce Court" flood the airwaves. The tabloids scream their titillating headlines; the evening magazine shows like "A Current Affair" provide nightly sensationalism (much of it based on stories that are far too old to be newsworthy but that still pack shock value); and even the more legitimate press have taken to running columns on "the news of the bizarre." To make things more confusing, the line between fact and fiction has been forever obscured with the advent of docudramas and pseudo-realistic shows like "America's Most Wanted." And a final trend is the expectation by the public that news of court proceedings be served in increasingly brief sound bites that ignore the complexity of the law.

Here and there coverage of courts has improved, or at least become more prominent. National Public Radio does an exemplary job of covering court news, offering far more than the traditional 10-second slug before moving on to sports and weather. National newspapers now present weekly columns or pages devoted to court news. Cable, notably CNN and the new Court TV (created by legal publisher Steven Brill, among others) has invented an entirely new market for the unedited proceedings of trials and legal proceedings.

Time will tell whether such coverage really improves the public's understanding of what the system is supposed to do. I'm not really sure, for example, what value there was in a recent *New York Times* article in which members of the bar and the general public critiqued the televised performance of prosecutor Moira K. Lasch in the William Kennedy Smith trial. Neither am I convinced of the value of "legal experts" who give instantaneous analysis of trial proceedings, though I myself must confess to having fantasized about becoming the John Madden or Frank Gifford of court coverage.

Some people might argue that the boom in criminal court coverage is healthy, that it enhances public knowledge of the workings of our judicial system. Personally, I find most of it frightening. As a society we have gone beyond healthy curiosity. Instead we are on a treadmill of misinformation and misunderstanding that not only raises the tension between judges and journalists, but seriously undermines the integrity of our entire criminal justice system.

Let's look at just one area of misinformation—the portrayal of judges and lawyers in the entertainment media. In the past judges suffered from incredible stereotyping. Most television and movie judges were white males in their 50s and 60s with snowy white hair and a grizzled countenance. They had the wisdom of Solomon and the patience of Job. Those who did not appear godlike were lampooned, such as the political-hack judge in "Miracle on 34th Street," who had to consult with his political guru to determine if Kris Kringle really was Santa Claus. Other judges appeared as sinister prisoners of a corrupt system. The judges in the film "The Star Chamber" secretly arranged for the execution of defendants whom they had to release because of legal technicalities. The judge in the Paul Newman classic "The Verdict" was in cahoots with the big-firm, insurance company defense lawyer. And the judge in the movie "And Justice for All" swallowed the end of a revolver and ate his lunch dangling from a ledge above the city!

To its credit, the entertainment industry in recent years has given audiences an increasingly broader view of the criminal justice system. "Hill Street Blues" was a breakthrough in "reality" television, giving audiences a snapshot of what the producers thought the criminal justice system actually looked like. It has been followed more recently by "L.A. Law," "Equal Justice," "Reasonable Doubt" and other "true-to-life" courtroom dramas. Some of these shows are indeed a bit more realistic in their portrayals of the system. Television and movie judges now come from various ethnic groups, are both men and women, old and young.

Still, in my opinion, there is no profession more maligned on television and film than judges and lawyers. Despite the advances in some areas, for example, we still have the well-intentioned but neurotic judge. Judge Harry Stone on television's "Night Court" fits that mold. Judge Stone does magic tricks, gives marital advice, befriends delinquents and simply tries to survive in an environment that is out of control. Fictionalized judges who aren't neurotic, it seems, are still incompetent, calloused or corrupt. Even in medical shows that poke fun at doctors, such as "M*A*S*H*," "St. Elsewhere," "Doctor, Doctor" and "Trapper John, M.D.," the doctors might be portrayed as eccentric "flakes," but they are undeniably highly competent. Not so for judges.

This is, however, a relatively trivial example of misconceptions. The stakes get higher. The most recent national and state polls indicate that approximately 75 percent of adult Americans know little to nothing about the functioning of our court systems. Almost half think that a criminal defendant must prove his or her innocence even though the basis of our Constitution is that a person is innocent until proven guilty. Four out of 10 people feel that courts are solely responsible for the high crime rate in the country, and almost the same number believe that delay in the system is a major problem.

Importantly, these misperceptions are not the result of direct contact with the courts; rather they are created from a combination of Hollywood dramas and radio, television and newspaper coverage. A mid-1980s Hearst Corporation survey asked adults: "Where do you most frequently get information about the courts?" The most frequent answers were television news, 54 percent; newspapers, 51 percent; radio news, 28 percent; television dramas at almost 20 percent; and magazines, 18 percent. Compare those figures to those for people who have had experience with the courts: been a juror, 6 percent; other personal court experiences, 6 percent; people you know who have been jurors, 9 percent; people you know who have had other court experiences, 10 percent. The Hearst survey concludes that "Americans are twice as likely to get information about courts from television drama as they are from people they know who have been jurors or had other court experiences."

The result of all this is not only a low public confidence level in our courts, but hostility toward them as well. It is a natural human tendency to be suspicious of something one does not understand, especially if it is a system with such power over our daily lives.

What can be done to rectify things? First, attorneys and judges must work to demystify the system. They must work with the media not only to enhance accuracy, but to produce educational programming for the public. Community forums, adult education, mock trials, public affairs television and radio—all should be used to inform about the justice system. If the public feels the system is open to its concerns, people will be more trusting of it.

Secondly, the news media should place more emphasis on actual court coverage. In this regard, as I said earlier, the advent of "real-time" court coverage by CNN and Court TV can be seen as a positive development. The benefit of such coverage is that the public can see that not every trial is exciting, that most are actually quite boring, and that they are not intended as entertainment in the manner of Perry Mason. Rather, trials are functions of government—mechanisms designed to obtain truth and forums for the resolution of disputes. No more and no less. In its dramas, Hollywood should attempt to show some modicum of respect for reality. I, for one, would appreciate it if the middle-aged, white-headed, wise, Caucasian judge were retired and replaced by people who reflect the diversity of our judiciary.

Unless at least some of these things are done, I fear the public will become increasingly intolerant of our criminal justice system and will demand ever more of its justice in sound bites and dramatic flourishes. That would be a great danger. Our system, as designed and tested by history, is about equal justice under the law and not, under any name, entertainment.

Thomas S. Hodson is a former trial judge and attorney in Athens, Ohio.

9

The Court Officer: Meet the Press

Rebecca Fanning

Not long ago a judge in a small town in Minnesota found himself deciding a custody case in which the children involved picketed the courthouse. They were afraid the judge would decide to return them to one of their parents, whom they claimed was abusive. What began as a local story quickly mushroomed into a national one, and since family court matters are highly confidential, this fascinating story of adolescents taking on the system put the judge in a very difficult situation: What could he possibly say to shed light on the situation without violating the judicial code of conduct?

I talked with the judge and asked him to explain the situation, his concerns and his judicial limits. After a lengthy discussion, I came back to him with a series of questions that have been useful to many judges with whom I have worked in Minnesota and elsewhere. They are:

Q: *What is the essential issue that has an impact on the public or that concerns the public in this situation?*

A: Every child deserves a safe, supportive home environment. That is the court's number-one priority.

Q: *What statement can I make that educates the public and fosters understanding of the difficult role of the judge?*

A: I have a great deal of empathy for these children and the difficult time they are going through. I have visited with them personally, and I have assured them that my first priority is making a decision in their best interests.

Q: *What action is being taken to address the public concern about the situation?*

A: Protecting the confidential relationship with the children prohibits me from talking about this particular case. In a situation like this one the judge calls on information and opinions from the involved persons and from professionals. Certain conditions and safeguards must be met before a family can be reunited. It is up to all of us to protect the best interests of our children.

Is this "spin doctoring"? Media manipulation? Not in my opinion. It is helping a judge, who otherwise would have spoken in legal jargon or stonewalled reporters, to give an interview that helps the public better understand the court system. I am the Minnesota state court system information officer—a job equivalent to the governor's press secretary—and my ability to act as a liaison between the courts and the media heightens the likelihood that the public will have the information needed to preserve and enhance an institution that is the cornerstone of democracy.

As the types of cases that come before the courts grow in number and complexity, so the relationship between judges and journalists becomes more important and, often, more strained. Consider the following examples of Minnesota cases and imagine the difficulties faced by judges and journalists in resolving them and communicating their impact on the public.

- An elderly man goes to court to be recognized as the decision-maker for his wife, who has been in a persistent vegetative state for more than a year. Against the man's wishes, the health-care professionals at the facility where she is hospitalized want to disconnect the life-support systems.
- A judge, after evaluating a defendant's criminal-history record and the immediate availability of jail space, releases a man who has been arraigned on charges of armed robbery. While awaiting trial, the man is arrested on charges of murder in another armed robbery.
- A judge sentences a man convicted of 13 charges of driving while intoxicated to the maximum jail time allowed under the state's sentencing guidelines. Citizen groups are outraged that the sentence is 13 months.

In Minnesota, I am the person whom judges call in these situations. I am also the person reporters call when judges won't talk with them. I am not a "handler"; neither am I a lawyer. I see my role as improving, not setting up additional barriers to, the communication between judges and journalists, and that means getting judges comfortable talking with reporters and helping journalists reach a more sophisticated level of understanding about the courts. Improving the working relationship between judges and journalists is crucial to public understanding, investment and involvement in the system. Indeed, judges have as much or more at stake as journalists do in seeing to it that stories about the courts are accurate and complete. As Woodrow Wilson put it: "So far as the individual is concerned, a constitutional government is as good as its courts. No better, no worse." My job is to make the courts work better by making sure the public understands what it is that judges do.

When I started the court information office in Minnesota in 1988, I interviewed more than 60 trial court- and appellate-level judges to find out what their foremost job concern was. Uniformly, they described working with the media as one of their most frustrating and fearsome tasks—and certainly one they tried to avoid. When asked for a few key words to describe journalists, judges came forward with "arrogant," "superficial" and "out to get us." Journalists, in turn, described judges as "arrogant," "bureaucratic" and "inaccessible." I interviewed more than a dozen print and broadcast reporters from around the state, in urban centers as well as small towns, and almost all said they found the system mysterious and the judges hard to reach.

Well, it wasn't hard to figure out where to start, and my experience since then has only confirmed the obvious: at all three levels of the state court system, when a story goes wrong it is all too often because judges have made themselves unavailable to journalists. To be fair, judges often feel constrained by the Code of Judicial Conduct, which admonishes them not to discuss a pending case, and each judge has to make his or her own determination as to what is appropriate to say to the media. But judges can abide by the spirit and the letter of this tenet and still answer basic questions raised by journalists on behalf of the public. In my experience, 99 percent of them are about process, scheduling, legal terms and concepts that need explanation or clarification. Inappropriate questions can easily be handled with an explanation of the code.

My strategy for solving this problem was equally obvious: to teach judges how to be more comfortable, in charge and effective in interviews; and to teach journalists the basics of the court system. The program was conducted over a two-year period, during which we conducted seminars in each of Minnesota's 10 judicial districts so that judges and court personnel interacted with local reporters about local concerns. The seminars were attended by 161 of the state's 260 judges, by a selected sampling of court administrators in each county who have regular contact with journalists, and by more than 200 reporters, editors and copy editors in print and broadcast media from around Minnesota. The judges met informally with journalists to discuss how well the courts provide information and how the system could be improved, and the judges also taught the classes on the role and function of the courts.

It worked. I saw attitudes changing before my eyes. After each of the sessions I asked judges and journalists what they learned about the other that surprised them. The overwhelming response from judges was their surprise that journalists really do want to get the story right. Journalists, in turn, expressed their surprise that these highly educated, articulate judges were intimidated by the media.

Underlying these observations, I believe, is one of the most interesting things about the relationship between judges and journalists: just how much they have in common—sometimes to their detriment. Both think the other has control in an interview, a perception that sets up a power struggle that is difficult to override. Both are used to being in charge, having people flex to accommodate them and knowing and setting the rules of a game that is mysterious to the uninitiated. Both appreciate the power of information and are motivated by a sense of right. In the case of journalists, their sense of right includes the hammer of the people's right to know; for judges, their sense of right includes the gavel governing a fair trial. The result, historically, has included some enormously complicated collisions of constitutional interpretation.

The point is that while judges and journalists often have similar goals, their work is governed by different institutional methods and values. Judges tend to be concerned with process, while journalists focus on outcome and impact. Judges are trained to build the foundation for an argument and lead the audience to the point. Journalists get to the point and then explain how they got there. It's simply the difference between inductive and deductive reasoning; however, it can cause a major communication problem. The difference in approach sets the stage for judges to believe that reporters have a preconceived notion about the story and are just out to prove their hypothesis. An understanding of these differences can take some of the mystery and confusion out of the communication process.

Similarly, a development that a journalist sees as newsworthy a judge might see as sensational. Judges forget or don't understand that journalists are seeking information their consumers need or want to know because it is out of the ordinary and/or has an impact on them—that is, it's news.

These professional differences of perception are for the best—together they can provide the public a clearer picture of how well its court system works, and ideally these tensions help to make the system work better. But that's only if judges and journalists pay attention to each other's needs.

Journalists, for instance, may wonder where judges are going with a particular story and get lost, confused and/or bored wondering when the judge will get to the point. If judges want to do their part to improve the accuracy of reporting, they need to be flexible enough to get to the point *first* so that the reporter knows what to listen for and what is significant. When I train judges to give an effective interview, I warn them that if they tell their story chronologically they provide more opportunities for the journalist to select what the judge may consider to be a wrong conclusion. Judges would be providing an important educational service— plus protecting their own interests—if they would visualize who is interested in a story and why. Just as a skilled attorney tries to understand and speak to a jury's concerns, a judge should take time to prepare for an interview by making a list of the audiences and what their questions are likely to be. Judges should explain, put into context and give common examples that aid understanding.

Journalists, in turn, would do well to understand that the basis of most of the frustration on the part of judges stems from their expectation that a reporter understands the system as well they do. While journalism has become increasingly specialized at some large newspapers, very few newspapers of any size and even fewer broadcast media have the luxury of having court-beat reporters. Often a reporter is literally thrown into a story at the last minute, ill prepared on that particular case and— like most members of the lay public—lacking even a basic understanding of the courts. Judges are deeply offended by this, though the best of them remember that their audience is the general public, which knows less about a particular case or the court system in general than a highly motivated but unprepared reporter. Judges should realize that reporters have a very limited window of time to get the story and to get it right, and that they are not "doing the reporter's job" by providing information necessary to the accurate reporting of a story.

As a former reporter, it sometimes surprises me just how poorly many people understand what it is journalists do. (That, unfortunately, is journalism's problem.) Judges, for example, frequently express frustration when they give a long interview and very little of it is used. They don't understand that reporters may approach a story from any of a number of different perspectives—testing a hypothesis, checking out a rumor, understanding something better—or they may not know what they are looking for until they find it. Fewer reporters today use the "Columbo" style of reporting, in which the element of surprise is an essential part of their style, and most can put judges at ease and get more cooperation just by telling them what the story is about, if the journalist knows. Coming from an environment in which the process of discovery allows them to get a sense of the direction of a line of questioning, judges feel uncomfortable and defensive when they don't know what a journalist's inquiry is driving at.

When a reporter calls me I always ask what the story is about, who else has been interviewed and generally what the other sources had to say. I have always gotten information from reporters that has helped me to help them get the story. Judges can do the same.

Whatever a journalist's style and tactics, I encourage judges to think of themselves as educators, with an opportunity to work with reporters to create understanding. As any educator knows, patience is part of the process, and when judges neglect it the result is almost always an error that a little greater accessibility might well have prevented. Often the error turns on a very basic, factual question that the judge could have answered easily and simply. If I have one piece of advice for judges who want to protect their good name and that of the judiciary, it would be to return journalists' calls without fail and to do it as quickly as possible. If a reporter is pursuing some incorrect information, the faster the contact is made the more quickly the faulty thinking can be corrected.

Journalists, judges and court information officers can improve their communication and working relationship in some relatively quick and easy ways. Knowing what I do about their interactions, I offer the following recommendations. Some may seem obvious—particularly to those who ply other beats—but among those who work the courts too few observe them:

- For high-profile cases, judges and journalists both benefit from a pretrial meeting during which they work out the ground rules for coverage, establish lines of communication and the logistical and institutional support systems necessary to assure the timely flow of information. At that meeting the judge should establish when she will be available for interviews and clarify what kinds of information she will and will not give, and journalists can voice their concerns about the ground rules and ask any questions they have about the background of the case. Set up systems and procedures for everything from fax and copying needs to reserved seating for journalists and sketch artists.

- Both judges and journalists should establish rapport with individuals within each system. Having a relationship with a couple of people you grow to trust gives you the latitude to ask questions, share information and gain a better understanding of each other's subculture. It is advantageous to be on speaking terms with as many judges/journalists as possible.

   The top complaint from judges at the Minnesota seminars was that they had never seen a reporter until a "sensational" story broke. Journalists might not find judges so inaccessible if they personally knew a few. These judges may be willing to serve as deep background sources, and they can also be your best advocate with other judges and court personnel.

- If your state has a court information officer, put him or her to work. The request of a judge or a journalist is top priority at my office. I time how quickly we respond to reporters' many and varied requests.

   Journalists should be aware of the kinds of information the court information officer and administrators can obtain and meet with them to find out what services and information are available. For journalists and the lay public I have written a 25-page consumer guide to the state courts, complete with charts that allow the reader to follow different kinds of cases through the court system. For judges I have a media-relations manual, and I am available at any time to advise them.

- Judges and journalists need to read and observe court coverage. Judges should pay attention to news trends and how court news is covered, as well as note bylines. Journalists can supplement their knowledge of the courts and current legal affairs issues.

In a sense, I now do formally what was done for many years, in Minnesota and elsewhere, by bench-bar-press councils. But where their work more closely resembled a negotiated cease-fire between combatants in the years after the Reardon Commission and the U.S. Supreme Court's various court-access rulings, mine seeks to exploit the peace, to further understanding in an age of increasing legal complexity.

Does it work? Here in Minnesota there are indications it does. Three years ago, when I first talked with judges about the press, they saw themselves as media victims. I made it my goal to foster an environment in which the one-upmanship among judges would switch from how many times they'd been burned to how effectively they had handled media interviews to meet their own communication objectives. I am beginning to see the balance of bragging shift to the latter side of the scale.

I was recently confronted with how different my approach must be when I got an unexpected call from "A Current Affair." I stunned a rather bristly researcher by not only answering her questions fully and undefensively but by immediately faxing background information and setting up an appointment with the judge she wanted to interview. I talked with the judge that day to help her tell her story in understandable terms. The reporter never showed up and has not returned my follow-up calls. I hope she survived the shock.

Rebecca Fanning is the court information officer for the Minnesota judiciary. She is a former public relations manager for the Twin Cities Star Tribune *and began her career as a reporter for United Press International.*

10

The Reporter II: Better Than Real Life

Edna Buchanan

Bullet-riddled bodies, orphaned babies, grim police controlling the chaos with yellow ropes: murder in Miami—as usual.

But this one had something no murder scene in Miami ever had before: a movie star.

Hollywood had come to the *Miami Herald* to shoot *Mean Season,* a movie starring Kurt Russell and Mariel Hemingway, with Russell portraying a police reporter. Some scenes would be shot at the newspaper, and the director had asked me to take Russell out on the police beat to prepare for his role.

It would be a learning experience for both of us.

I was not thrilled. I like working alone and did not want to turn my beat into a traveling dog-and-pony show. This is not entertainment, I told myself, this is real life, serious business. In addition I had little faith in Hollywood's dedication to reality. When scenes for *Absence of Malice* were filmed at the *Herald* years earlier, Sally Field had accompanied a reporter on a story to prepare for her role. Sally quickly became bored and departed. We never saw her again, except on the big screen.

So I was surprised and slightly annoyed one afternoon when Kurt Russell called and asked to come by the newsroom. Sure, I said, warning that if a story broke I might be gone before he arrived.

A short time later a stranger appeared at my desk. "Hi," he said, "I'm Kurt Russell."

He looked rumpled enough to be a reporter: gold-rimmed spectacles, faded blue jeans, tennis shoes and a T-shirt from a small-town Colorado bar. I had seen one of his films, *Silkwood,* but I would not have recognized him now. His entrance was so unobtrusive that no one else even looked up. "Where's your entourage?" I asked. He had none.

Minutes later, as if on cue, a call came: a double murder. The movie star was surprised that in spite of deadline urgency, we had to fight bumper-to-bumper traffic to reach the crime scene. "It never even occurred to me that you have to deal with the stupid everyday things like rush hour."

The neighborhood was residential. A young married couple had been shot to death, murdered in their own home. One eyewitness: their toddler son, 15 months old. The orphan was found clinging to his mother's body, drenched in her blood and wailing. An older brother, age three, was safe in nursery school. No one had picked up the older child, so school officials notified a relative, who went to the house to find out why the parents did not answer the telephone. He discovered the bodies.

The crowd was mostly neighborhood residents. We mingled with the morbidly curious, the police and the press. The murderer had escaped undetected, but Kurt Russell did not. Since I would not have recognized the actor in a crowd, I didn't expect anyone else to. Wrong.

As the star absorbed the real-life drama, the atmosphere began to change. A man in the crowd stared. Some young girls gawked and giggled. An irate young woman, about to slam her door to avoid my questions, paused, eyes fixed on the face over my shoulder. Her expression softened, her lips parted. A middle-aged woman in Red Cross shoes forgot the sheer horror of the crime and trotted after us in hot pursuit of Russell's autograph.

Gut reaction masked, he pleasantly complied with the request as the woman burbled praise for *Silkwood*. She clutched her little trophy.

A cry echoed through the crowd: "Do you know who that is?" Fellow suburbanites slaughtered in their home were suddenly forgotten. A TV news crew caught on. Their camera swung into a 180-degree turn. Dead bodies and babies forgotten, the film crew stampeded after the star, clamoring for an interview. The crowd followed.

Police officers assigned to crowd control at the crime scene looked puzzled. Only moments earlier they had to force people to stand behind the yellow ropes. Now they were no longer necessary. The crowd had run off in pursuit of some stranger. We dashed for the car and made our getaway.

I was surprised. So was Kurt Russell. He had underestimated his appeal. Even if recognized, he had expected to be ignored because of the sensational events at the murder scene. Wrong again.

I thought my job was the real stuff, gritty, true life-and-death drama, but to most people what they see in darkened movie theaters is far more compelling. They are fascinated by a re-creation of life, somehow bigger, better and far more appealing than the real thing.

Russell later told costar Mariel Hemingway: "I guarantee you that if somebody was lying in the street bleeding and you came up, they'd forget the emergency. The victim would be crying 'God! Get me help! My leg's been cut off.... Wait, wait a minute. You're Mariel Hemingway!'"

Later events proved him right.

The crew was shooting a murder scene on the beach at dawn. Coincidentally, a real-life murder was unfolding on the beach that early morning. The scenario began late the night before. A young couple had been drinking wine and cuddling in a car parked near the water. A stranger emerged from the shadows, announced he was a police officer and ordered the young man to step out of the car. When he did, the stranger battered him to death with a baseball bat.

The killer kidnapped the girl. She was raped, driven aimlessly around the city, then left in a strange neighborhood.

Police took her back to the murder scene as they tried to piece the story together. The teenager sobbed inconsolably, with good reason. Her date had been brutally murdered. She had been abducted and violated. A policeman happened to mention the film crew shooting nearby. The victim's sobs subsided and she asked if they thought she could get to meet Kurt Russell? The cops said they would ask.

The actor readily agreed, after being told what had happened. He sat and counseled the girl for some time.

Counseled? Who needs a rape counselor when you have Kurt Russell?

Edna Buchanan is a Pulitzer Prize-winning police reporter for the Miami Herald. *This vignette is adapted from* Never Let Them See You Cry, *Random House, 1992.*

III

The Culture of Crime

11

Nervous in the Naked City

Howard Rosenberg

Beware! Time to buy that Uzi and barricade yourself.

There's a very good chance that you will be raped or sexually assaulted, taken hostage, mugged, robbed at gunpoint, tortured, mutilated, maimed, fatally beaten, shot, hanged, smothered, drowned, decapitated, knifed, strangled, poisoned, impaled on bamboo stakes, disemboweled, pushed out of a 10-story window, bombed or bitten in the neck by a vampire masquerading as your next-door neighbor.

At least that's the impression you get from watching television.

"Naked City," the classic New York cop series that ran on ABC from 1958 to 1963, had this famous signature: "There are eight million stories in the naked city...." And now, as it turns out, eight million TV programs that tell them.

The mean, perilous society that TV overwhelmingly depicts, in too many series, too many movies and too many newscasts, is one decimated by crime and dominated by hardened criminals.

An off-duty officer up against an armed bank robber, a new designer drug causing a multitude of overdoses, and a young boy kidnapped and held for ransom are featured on "Top Cops."

Typical was a recent newscast on KCAL-TV in Los Angeles. The first six stories were about multiple murders, the seventh about a fire, the eighth about "cemeteries that abuse the dead." What about stations that, by fueling public panic, abuse the airwaves?

One would prefer that TV, rather than frighten and polarize America, use its stereophonic voice to bring the nation together by uplifting and enlightening. Instead, its noisiest message is that appearing on the street unaccompanied by pit bulls or not building a moat around your home for protection can cost you your life.

That is what TV is preaching, despite statistics showing a steady decline in the chances of most Americans becoming crime victims. According to the Bureau of Justice Statistics, crimes against persons aged 12 and over fell 3.6 percent from 1989 to 1990. And although the number of violent crimes rose 3.3 percent for that period, the Bureau says, there were still only 34.2 violent crimes per 1,000 persons in the West, 31.1 in the South, 30.5 in the Midwest and 21.8 in the Northeast. Statistically, then, roughly only one of 30 Americans is victimized by violent crime. That rate may be horrific and intolerable to us as a society— especially if we're the one in 30—but it pales against the blinding neon of criminal carnage, both real and fictional, spewing from TV up to 24 hours a day.

"Silk Stalkings," a new late-night "Crime Time After Prime Time" series about a team of homicide detectives specializing in high-profile crimes of passion, will premiere Thursday.

Are we talking about felonious sneering or snickering here? Homicidal taunting or teasing? No. Dr. George Gerbner, former dean of the Annenberg School for Communication at the University of Pennsylvania, is pretty much on target in defining violence on television as the "overt expression of physical force (with or without a weapon, against self or others) compelling action against one's will on pain of being hurt and/or killed, or threatened to be so victimized as part of the plot."

Increasingly, violent crime is part of the plot, as TV programs continue to bypass the ordinary and define society by the deviant. That TV is constantly re-excavating itself was vividly affirmed with the arrival in 1991 of an NBC movie titled "The Return of Eliot Ness." Thus in a sense, TV's present crime wave is an artifact of its own archaeology, a renovated and reprocessed fossil from an element of broadcast culture that itself is rooted in a theatrical crime-movie genre nearly as old as the one-reeler. Offering the action and conflict deemed essential to the visual medium, crime has been an ingredient of prime time practically from TV's arrival as popular entertainment, ranging from the papa/daughter detecting of ABC's trifling "Crime With Father" in 1951–52 to the long-running "Perry Mason" on CBS to NBC's eternal "Dragnet" to such heavier weights as NBC's "Police Story" anthology of the mid-1970s and "Hill Street Blues" in the 1980s. In the 1990–91 season, moreover, ABC had a fling even with a *musical* crime series, the short-lived, too rarely melodic "Cop Rock" from "Hill Street Blues" creator Steven Bochco.

Surveying today's TV landscape, though, it becomes obvious that never before has the medium from bottom to top been, well, so criminal.

"48 Hours" joins men and women across the nation who are fed up with crime and are resisting it by learning the art of self-defense, becoming street fighters and forming patrol groups to take back their streets.

"Television would have no power if it did not have viewers eager to consume its message," says author William F. Fore, visiting lecturer in communications at Yale University Divinity School. Carrying this further, if the public weren't fascinated by crime, then the entrepreneurs of television wouldn't air it, cable wouldn't have a Court TV network that airs trials live and uncut, and CNN may not have devoted huge chunks of airtime to the rape trial of William Kennedy Smith. It appears, in fact, that TV has nurtured its own crime-devouring monster—the viewer—and now must feed the ravenous appetite it helped create.

Thus, although prime time and early evening tabloid programs get most of the attention, all of TV is getting to be prime time for crime, including the daytime soap operas that we associate more often with sex than with slaughter. For example, here are excerpts of a single week's story lines for five network soap operas:

- "At her attempted-murder trial, Janet went on the witness stand and said Natalie always hated and ridiculed her."—"All My Children."
- "Bill told Faison and Leopold that he had to kill Harlan because he was loyal to Robert and that he then shoved both bodies into the river."— "General Hospital."
- "Julie saw Roger and Jean argue before Blake discovered Jean's body floating in the country club pool."—"Guiding Light."
- "Before Warren turned himself in, he realized Craig may have shot Mason."—"Santa Barbara."
- "Ceara and Jeremy were there for Matt when he testified against his stepfather, the Rev. Ford, who was sentenced to 25 years in prison for abusing Matt and for molesting and raping girls."—"Loving."

Add to these a spate of syndicated daytime talk hours, led by "The Oprah Winfrey Show," "Donahue," "Geraldo" and "Sally Jessy Raphael," which increasingly sell themselves to viewers with themes ranging from sensational crimes to serial killers and their spouses who still love them.

Oprah to guest: "OK, so you know now you're living with a homicidal maniac. What happened? He got rid of the body, obviously. "

Add also such syndicated crime-driven tabloid series as "Hard Copy," "A Current Affair" and "Inside Edition," which stations often adjoin to local or network newscasts. In doing so they blur the distinction between these genres, creating a block of crime-colored programming leading forth to the prime-time hours that themselves have seen an explosion of so-called "reality" series that either re-enact actual crimes in a documentary style, and invite viewers to phone in tips on suspects, or use the camera to zero in on the activities of law enforcement authorities.

From a programmer's perspective, the irresistible appeal of a "reality" series is its potentially high return on a relatively low investment. Yet all of these series, including NBC's especially popular "Unsolved Mysteries," may have been motivated, at least subliminally, by the success of "60 Minutes," whose most spectacular stories are about crime cases that leave behind loose ends like a trail of bread crumbs. Attempting to knot these loose ends, "Unsolved Mysteries" claims that its dramatic re-enactments of unsolved crimes have prompted viewer call-ins to its hot line that have resulted in scores of these cases being solved.

"Unsolved Mysteries" premiered in 1987. Seeing that crook catching and crime busting were going to be big business, Fox Broadcasting got into the act itself a year later by putting on the air "America's Most Wanted," a program with a format almost identical to the NBC series, and one claiming to have been instrumental in the capture of more than 170 fugitives, including one murder suspect who was nabbed 27 minutes after his profile aired.

Profiles of a Houston man wanted for the murder of a security guard on New Year's Eve, a paroled rapist who allegedly attacks again and an illegal alien wanted for the murder of his girlfriend are featured on "America's Most Wanted. "

Given the high-profile success of "Unsolved Mysteries" and "America's Most Wanted," and the obvious entertainment underpinnings of TV vigilantism, it was inevitable that smaller-scale imitators would spring up, each armed with suspect lists supplied by local law enforcement agencies and their own hot lines for viewers to call. Many of these programs, such as "Philadelphia's Most Wanted," have originated on local cable, giving them a populist flavor. An even larger trend has been the proliferation of "most wanted"-style segments in newscasts across the nation, as local stations continue to chip away at journalism with the sharp edges of entertainment.

Just as local stations have sought to capitalize, predictably so have NBC's and Fox's network competitors. Hence, the 1990 arrival of the CBS series "Top Cops"—with its own re-enactments of "stories from the case files of police officers from across the country"—was almost a given. As was the 1991 emergence of "FBI: The Untold Stories," an ABC series merging agents' own flashbacks, newsreel footage and still more of those glossy re-enactments of actual cases, all with the purpose of dramatizing the Bureau's "relentless battle against crime in every sector."

When it comes to being relentless, however, the FBI is a blind, lumbering yak compared with TV executives hot on the trail of green. Even before ordering up "America's Most Wanted," for example, Fox's very own junior G-men had given a trial to something called "Cops" in advance of making it a full-fledged series in 1989 that would be the model in 1991 for ABC's "American Detective."

In one investigation, detectives confiscate everything from the home of an alleged drug dealer who has marijuana plants all over his house. In a second case, snitches help in the apprehension of another alleged drug dealer. And in a third, an informant and a drug dog sniff out an alleged narcotic dealer.

"No scripts, no actors, no phony endings—just cops." That's how Fox advertised a hybrid that somehow crossed Frederick Wiseman with Geraldo Rivera in its use of video-vérité techniques to hyperactively record the work of police forces across the nation and even in the Soviet Union.

"No actors, no scripts...what is seen is real." That's how ABC described its own "American Detective" two years later. Stalking "Cops," "American Detective" pairs human interest and human tragedy, traveling from city to city in quest of telegenic police officers living their lives and enforcing the law in ways that will keep viewers pinned to their sets. Working closely with cops, it becomes their companion, shadowing them out in their homes, in their station houses, in their patrol cars and on the streets where they work. The action and unpredictability of "Cops" and "American Detective" make these series transfixing on a visceral level, their intimate footage of murder investigations, prostitution stings and drug busts inflating sideshow subcultures into main events. Even when all of this happens so chaotically that you don't quite comprehend what's happening—with cops hitting fast and rounding up suspects in a blur—you're seduced and energized by the process.

Moreover, unlike the bulk of prime-time crime programs, which give a distorted picture by dwelling on victims from the upper strata while largely ignoring violence in low-income neighborhoods, these series accompany police into the urban cesspools and armpits of society where the majority of crime occurs. And in doing so, they validate and attach human faces to statistics that show blacks and Latinos as being much more likely than whites to be victims of crime.

A segment of "Cops" featuring a woman who allegedly stabbed her boyfriend, both of whom have AIDS, shed light on a new crime trend recognized by law enforcement: selling AIDS-treatment medication on the street in exchange for heroin and cocaine.

But no actors? No scripts? What is seen is real? Well, surely not always.

Just as re-enactments deployed by tabloids and other crime series dangerously fuse fact and fantasy even when labeled, so does the unnarrated, voyeuristic style of "Cops" and "American Detective" obscure the line separating what's real and what isn't.

For example, who among us would not become an actor when in the presence of a TV camera close enough to record every facial tic? Some early scenes from "Cops" serve as examples, including one where the camera closed tight on a Florida sheriff's deputy kissing his wife after a day at the office, another where a male officer proposed to a female officer on a boat in a lake. Not putting on a bit for the lens? And wouldn't a camera practically sitting on their noses alter the behavior of participants on both sides in a police interrogation on "American Detective"?

Meanwhile, is it any accident that John Bunnel, the handsome Portland, Oregon, narcotics cop that "American Detective" has spent so much time with, just happens to be at once heroic, sensitive and sympathetic, as if summoned from central casting? Or that "American Detective" arrived almost on cue as an image-correcting antidote to the notorious case of Rodney G. King, the African-American motorist whose savage beating by Caucasian Los Angeles police officers as he lay on the ground was captured by an amateur with a camcorder and indelibly stamped on our consciousness through repeated showing on TV?

Should they occur, you'll see no incidents of police brutality on "American Detective" or "Cops," for a weakness of both series is that in order for them to ensure police cooperation, they must glorify law officers even while humanizing them through intimate television exposure.

The "American Detective" and "Cops" phenomenon has not been lost on TV's snootier crowd either. "Hit the streets with real-life private eyes as they investigate everything from murders to kidnappings," reads a watching-the-detectives program note for a documentary series on the Arts & Entertainment Network, a major cable system calling itself an alternative to public television in the areas of culture and refinement.

It's prime time, too, that's being hit not only by a barrage of crime via regular series but also by movie after movie featuring murder or other forms of mayhem as nearly every sensational crime case worthy of a newspaper headline—from the "Hillside Strangler" to the "Night Stalker"—touches off a feeding frenzy among predatory Hollywood producers fighting over rights to make the inevitable exploitative docudrama. Nearly all will end up being formulaic, depicting the usual catching, trying and convicting of a criminal while conveying nothing beyond the compassion for the victim and contempt for the perpetrator that you felt going in.

The riveting, fact-based drama recounts the tragedy of a family ripped apart in the aftermath of a father's murder and the near-fatal attack on his wife. As she struggles to recover physically, she is psychologically and emotionally torn by mounting evidence that the killer is a member of her own family.

When it comes to such movies, at least prime time is no longer discriminating as often against female crooks. Prominent among the many heavily promoted TV crime movies that surfaced during the November 1991 ratings sweeps, for example, were a combined eight from ABC, NBC and CBS about women accused of committing serious offenses: Six were charged with murder, another with dealing drugs and another with kidnapping.

This may have been a welcome departure from the weary, stereotyping practice of portraying females mostly as victims. But it also dramatized TV's ever-growing role as the nation's criminal archive, a sort of round-the-clock *Crime Magazine* of the airwaves and repository for lawlessness.

To what end ultimately? Certainly no beneficial one, if you believe, as some do, that TV has contributed to a national paranoia about crime far out of proportion to the actual threat. According to researcher emeritus Gerbner, the more television one watches the more likely that person will be to distrust the world around him, and the more likely to buy a gun, install more locks and obtain watchdogs. In a sense, then, many Americans are being held hostage by their own fear in an environment that is dangerously tense and volatile. Given the inclination of self-serving politicians to exploit and distort the crime issue to curry favor with voters—and the public's relatively easy access to guns in the United States—it's easy to see how the fear itself can be as great a national problem as the crime that generates it.

As Andy Griffith's nervous pal Barney Fife once observed: "Anxiety magnifies fearsome objects."

Scanning the TV listings, meanwhile, you note that J.L. McCabe is investigating a model's death on "Jake and the Fatman"; Tony Scali is matching wits with a mugger while investigating the slaying of an elderly woman in her home on "The Commish"; a game show host is accused of murder on "Matlock"; Deborah Harry is playing a telephone-sex operator whose number may be up when she's stalked by a serial killer on Showtime; and Telly Savalas is narrating "Perfect Crimes," a CBS special about actual crimes "committed with planning and forethought but unraveled by the smallest detail."

Perhaps, through television, it's America that's unraveling. Not to worry, though, for as the naked city rages outside, you're sitting in front of the set watching your favorite crime show.

A can of beer in one hand, a can of mace in the other.

Howard Rosenberg is a Pulitzer Prize-winning television critic for the Los Angeles Times.

12

Kids and Crime

Michele Magar

On a typical day in America in 1989, more than 92,000 children were incarcerated in public and private institutions; juvenile facilities had more than 750,000 admissions in the course of the year. These record numbers occurred while the number of children in the population was decreasing and represent a nearly 20 percent increase over four years in the proportion of American children held in custody.

While the number of incarcerated children was going up, the rate of youth arrests for serious crimes declined by 17 percent from 1979 to 1989. "Overall, juvenile crime peaked in 1975 and has been dropping ever since," says Hunter Hurst, director of the National Center for Juvenile Justice in Pittsburgh.

So why are more kids being locked up when fewer are being arrested? One reason is pressure from a public that believes juvenile crime is out of control. Eighty-two percent of Americans surveyed in the summer of 1991 believed youth crime had gone up in their state in the last three years, with the majority stating it had increased greatly. Interestingly, only 27 percent reported that juvenile crime had increased in *their* neighborhoods. The second statistic is a more accurate reflection of juvenile crime trends because it's based on what people know, not what they think, says Ira Schwartz, director of the University of Michigan's National Center for the Study of Youth Policy, which commissioned the survey.

Schwartz, who also headed the Justice Department's Office of Juvenile Justice and Delinquency Prevention from 1979 to 1981, believes with Hurst that the news media are at least partly to blame for the public's misperceptions about juvenile crime. By focusing coverage on violent youth crime, they say, the media keep alive the notion that violent acts are skyrocketing and constitute the most common type of juvenile offense. In fact, only 5 to 10 percent of juvenile crime involves violence.

The media's devotion to reporting violent crime holds true for adult crime as well. Harry L. Marsh, a criminology professor at Indiana State University in Terre Haute, has written that overrepresentation of crimes of violence committed by offenders of all ages is a common finding of content-analysis studies of American newspapers. Marsh's own survey of five major papers in Texas found a 4-1 ratio of violent-to-property crime stories, while official statistics revealed a crime ratio of 1 to 9. The most commonly cited reason for this discrepancy is also the most obvious: it sells newspapers. Says Marsh, "I called editors and was told, 'We write what the public wants to read.'"

While the public's thirst for sensational crime stories may provide the impetus for skewed crime coverage, Marsh says that the way most crime reporters cover their beats virtually guarantees an emphasis on violent crime. "Reporters are thinly scattered," he says. "They don't have time to go out and get crime stories firsthand. Usually there's only one or two reporters to cover the entire crime beat, and most crime coverage is done by rookie reporters." The result is that reporters over-rely on police sources, a practice that allows authorities to act as gatekeepers. "What gets reported, except from court documents, comes from police," says Marsh. "Police actually control what the newspapers get." Reporting on violent crime makes police look good, Marsh adds, because police solve a far higher percentage of homicides and sexual assaults than property crimes.

But distorted news coverage isn't the only explanation for the public's misconceptions about juvenile crime. Politicians also fuel the public's belief that crime by children is soaring. "Juvenile crime generates fear, and anything that generates fear is marketable," Hurst says. "Policy doesn't have to deal with crime, it just has to deal with fear." As an example, he cites Pennsylvania lawmakers' decision to prosecute children accused of homicide in adult criminal court. "That doesn't deal with prevention or control; it only acts after the fact," he says. "Homicide is an act of passion 70 percent of the time. But the law is a stroke of political genius in dealing with the fears of Pennsylvania residents."

The public's fear of juvenile crime, whipped into a frenzy by the government's war on drugs, has fueled the "get tough" policy toward youth crime that has swept the nation. Most commonly, this takes the form of legislation that makes it easier to prosecute children in adult criminal court. Ten states have lowered the upper age of juvenile court jurisdiction to 15 or 16. Thirty-two states allow children charged with certain violent offenses to be tried in adult court, and nine give prosecutors the option to file charges for serious offenses in adult court.

A new juvenile crime initiative announced last November by Washington, D.C., Mayor Sharon Pratt Kelly is typical of actions taken by many states in the last decade. Kelly wants to lower from 15 to 14 the age at which children charged with felonies can be transferred to adult court, and wants to change the criteria for transfer from "reasonable prospects for rehabilitation" to "interest of public welfare and protection of the public security." Kelly would also replace the two-year cap on juvenile sentencing with indeterminate terms and create a secure juvenile facility for serious offenders.

Reporters who have the time and desire to write about juvenile delinquency by covering more than the most high-profile youth crimes have an abundance of good stories from which to choose. However, making sense of the juvenile justice system is impossible without understanding the theoretical framework that gives the system its logic—and is a story in itself.

The nation's first statute establishing a separate court for juveniles was enacted by the Illinois legislature in 1899. By 1945, every state and federal jurisdiction, as well as most European countries, had created their own juvenile justice system. American proponents of juvenile court argued that the principle of crime and punishment was inappropriate for children. Instead, children were to be treated and rehabilitated by the state acting as a kindly substitute parent. Since juvenile judges were meant to focus on the child's welfare and court procedures were not meant to be adversarial, the procedural rights available to adults were considered unnecessary and even counterproductive.

Then, in 1967, the U.S. Supreme Court declared the system hadn't worked. The case involved a writ for habeas corpus brought on behalf of 15-year-old Gerald Francis Gault, who had been sentenced to Arizona's State Industrial School until he reached 21 on a charge of making a lewd telephone call to a neighbor. The Court noted that an adult convicted of the same offense would have faced a maximum penalty of a $5 to $50 fine, or a jail term of two months.

The High Court ruled that the Constitution's 14th Amendment affords children at risk of incarceration the right to counsel, notice of charges, the privilege against self-incrimination and the right to cross-examine witnesses. Writing for the majority, Justice Abe Fortas characterized Gault's adjudication as a summary procedure and noted that "Under our Constitution, the condition of being a boy does not justify a kangaroo court."

In subsequent cases the Court found that proof beyond a reasonable doubt was required to convict children during delinquency hearings, and that the protection against double jeopardy applied to delinquency cases. But the Court stopped short of finding that children were entitled to trials by jury, for fear of turning juvenile proceedings into full-fledged adversarial procedures and putting "an effective end to what has been the idealistic prospect of an intimate, informal protective proceeding." [*McKeiver v. Pennsylvania,* (1971)].

The Court's refusal to completely abandon the notion that juvenile courts strive for rehabilitation rather than punishment is key to understanding the law's tolerance for a system that commonly sentences children accused of minor crimes to longer terms than they would have faced as adults. "If the challenge is to stabilize and bring growth to the child, that might take longer," says juvenile court Judge David Grossman of Cincinnati. "The system is based on the assumption that the court should act as a kindly parent," agrees Schwartz. "The reality is that the court acts as a sledgehammer: It's extremely punitive under the guise of being treatment-oriented."

The juvenile court's purported goal of rehabilitation has also been used to counter the charge that the system is racist. Statistics released by the Department of Justice show that compared to white children minority youth are disproportionately arrested for youth crimes; are less likely to have their cases handled informally; are more likely to be waived to adult criminal court; are more likely to be detained prior to trial for the same offense; are more likely to be incarcerated after trial; and are less likely to receive probation. Justice Department data also reveal a trend toward segregation in youth facilities: Minority youth make up the majority of prisoners in public facilities, while white youth predominate in private ones.

Yet a study conducted by Delbert S. Elliott at the University of Colorado in Boulder indicates that minority youth are no more likely to engage in crime than are white youth. Elliott's National Youth Survey is a confidential, self-reporting tool that measures children's involvement in crime. His writings suggest that social class and social condition may explain the racial disparities in the government's statistics on juveniles. According to Elliott, social factors may influence a child's ability to avoid apprehension and arrest; may determine whether a child receives legal and parental support from arrest through sentencing; and may affect a child's attitude and behavior toward the juvenile justice system.

In addition, the juvenile court's mission to provide individually tailored rehabilitation for young offenders creates the opportunity for differential treatment based on race, says Barry Feld, a law professor at the University of Minnesota: "Juvenile judges take social circumstances into account; they consider factors like poverty and the number of parents a kid has. That puts minority kids at greater risk for more severe sentences," because judges may reason that disadvantaged children need more help.

The system breaks down, according to Feld, because children are incarcerated in institutions that don't offer meaningful rehabilitation. "You can call them industrial training schools or state rehabilitation homes, but they're youth prisons," Feld says. "They're comparable to minimum- or medium-security adult prisons."

The punitive nature of the juvenile justice system makes it imperative that children be represented by attorneys, Feld argues, but despite the right to counsel guaranteed them under *Gault*, children often are unrepresented. In three of six states he studied, Feld found that nearly half or more children did not have lawyers. He adds that other studies he's seen show that children are represented in other jurisdictions between 22 to 45 percent of the time, with representation typically low in rural areas. The reason is that children often waive their right to counsel. "Judges tell kids, 'Of course you can have a lawyer, but you don't need one because I'm here to look after you,'" Feld says. "It takes a courageous kid to say to a judge, 'I don't trust you—I want a lawyer to represent me.'"

Perhaps more disturbing, Feld discovered that children represented by attorneys are more likely to receive longer sentences than children who waive their right to counsel. He thinks several factors contribute to his finding. For one, he says, "Juvenile court lawyers are largely incompetent and a threat to their clients. Juvenile court is not the kind of place attorneys regard as the pinnacle of their careers—it's the Siberia." But there is a second, more sinister explanation: "Judges are punishing kids who want attorneys. They think they're acting in the best interests of the child and take it as a personal affront when the child says 'I don't trust you.' And some judges think if a kid has a lawyer, the kid's rights are protected so they can sentence him to the max. Also, judges sometimes prejudge cases. If they think they're going to give a serious sentence, they'll recommend a lawyer so the record is covered and they can give a severe sentence." Feld adds that judges are also under pressure to keep their dockets moving and hold the system's costs down.

Although he's troubled by these findings, Feld believes that children deserve effective representation, and that the only way to guarantee it is to make their right to counsel unwaivable: "In every other area of the law, kids are considered incompetent. They can't write a contract, they can't vote, but they can waive their constitutional right to counsel."

Many who believe in the benevolent nature of juvenile court disagree. "If I had to tell my own child, I'd advise him not to have a lawyer," says Hunter Hurst. "The system is best approached by not denying what you've done. The intention is to rehabilitate—it's not like in adult court, where they stick it to you."

However, the intent behind juvenile courts denies children three rights guaranteed adults: the right to bail, a jury and a public trial. Mark Soler, who heads the Youth Law Center in San Francisco, thinks children should be entitled to all three. "Bail would eliminate detention for minor offenses," he says, and "many children could be released on their own recognizance like adults are." Soler also believes children should have access to juries: "Most public defenders feel their kids would have a better shot in front of a jury. Many juvenile court judges get hardened because they see so many cases."

Juvenile Court Judge David Grossman thinks the opposite: "Juries would give children no greater degree of justice. It's likely a jury will be tougher than a judge," he says, and he adds that juries would "jam up" the process by slowing the disposition of cases. However, Grossman agrees with Soler that reporters should be allowed in juvenile courts. "It's a good check on the system," he says, "a way to make sure the system is working." While juvenile judges do not have to allow reporters into their courtrooms, he says, it is not uncommon for them to do so. Feld also advocates opening juvenile courtrooms to reporters, saying that "confidentiality serves no purpose. In rural areas, everyone knows who's in trouble, and in urban areas there's anonymity."

Feld, in fact, believes the juvenile court system should be abolished. "There's no reason not to use the same system as adults," he says. "When kids come before the courts, they can still be sentenced more leniently and to separate institutions."

The juvenile justice subject about which it is easiest to find consensus is the separation of children from adult prisoners. It's difficult to argue against the somber statistics that frame the issue: Children housed with adult prisoners commit suicide eight times more often than their peers at all-youth facilities; they are also five times more likely to be sexually assaulted, and twice as likely to be beaten by guards. People also line up behind removing children from adult facilities because it's become public policy. In 1974 Congress passed the Juvenile Justice and Delinquency Prevention Act, which conditioned receipt of federal funds to states' removal of two classes of children from adult jails as well as youth detention centers and training schools: children accused of status offenses (offenses that are not illegal if committed by adults, such as running away or truancy), and children who have broken no laws but are in state custody because they are dependent, neglected or abused.

The law also mandated that youth incarcerated in adult facilities have no sound and sight contact with adult prisoners, and this is where problems arose. After hearing testimony that jail administrators used isolation wings, drunk tanks or abandoned areas of jails with little staff supervision to comply with the law's requirement for sight and sound separation, Congress amended the law in 1980 to require that children be removed from adult facilities, with some exceptions for rural areas that would end after 1993.

Although the law has had some impact, tens of thousands of children continue to be admitted to adult jails. Justice Department records show that juvenile admissions to adult jails declined from 105,366 in fiscal year 1983 to 65,263 in fiscal 1988. The government had no figures on the number of children admitted to the 3,570 police lockups across the country. In 1988, the Justice Department reported that four states and the District of Columbia were in full compliance with the law. Another 33 states were deemed to be mostly or substantially in compliance; 10 states were not in compliance but nonetheless received waivers enabling them to continue to receive federal funds; and three states chose not to participate.

Some advocates are worried that progress on removing children from adult jails could be stalled by the Bush Administration's recent relaxation of regulations implementing the act. Regulations require that jails have different staff and program areas for children. However, in 1991 the Justice Department granted a waiver to Wisconsin, which uses the same staff to work with adults and children, albeit on different shifts. The department also sent notices to the states informing them that the regulations were being changed in ways that would allow other states to follow Wisconsin's lead.

Soler says the waiver guts the regulations' intent to make jurisdictions provide children with specialized personnel rather than jail guards and will have the effect of making it easier for authorities to continue to house children and adults in the same facilities. To avoid this result, Soler says the Youth Law Center is considering a lawsuit against the federal government for not allowing public comment on the changes in the regulations, as required by law.

Robert Sweet Jr., administrator of the Office of Juvenile Justice and Delinquency Prevention, counters that the changes are minor and therefore don't come under the requirement for public comment. And he says Wisconsin's waiver does not represent any slippage in the federal government's commitment to enforce the law: "It's an honest difference of opinion about how laws apply. No other states are doing what Wisconsin has done. Sometimes, for advocates, there can be a fear that the government has a lack of commitment or is going back on previous policies."

"That's exactly what it is," Soler says. "It's the federal government weakening guidelines, allowing practices that will allow kids to be held in adult jails across the country. Maine and other states are already talking about doing the same thing as Wisconsin."

Although the press did not create the defects that riddle our society's response to juvenile crime, it bears at least some responsibility for making virtually impossible a national debate on how to improve the juvenile justice system. By focusing on the most serious types of youth crime, the press has done nothing to dissuade the public that juvenile crime is soaring, and that perception fuels public hunger for a punitive response.

However, the press cannot be faulted for covering what its audience wants, and there is no question that sensational crime stories attract readers.

There are two ways to address the problem. First, reporters and editors should make sure that at least some of the stories about violent crime committed by children include information about how typical that kind of crime is, and whether it's on the increase. Secondly, journalists should counterbalance their coverage of violent youth crime with occasional investigative pieces that examine particular aspects of the juvenile justice system, such as recidivism rates for different types of programs or evidence of differential treatment by race.

Journalists should also press for access to juvenile courts. By agreeing not to publish the names of juveniles, as David Grossman suggests (and as journalists usually do), the press can address the legitimate concern for children's privacy and simultaneously provide accountability for the juvenile court system.

Finally, any reform of the system itself will have to begin with the acknowledgment that despite its goals the system is punitive, not rehabilitative, and journalists have a large role to play here too. Once this point is established, it becomes ludicrous for society to deny children the rights guaranteed adults, or to hold them hostage to adult intentions. States, for example, might be encouraged to close training schools and large detention centers in favor of community-based alternatives that provide a well-coordinated array of services that include education and vocational training, substance-abuse treatment and medical intervention. Massachusetts took this step in 1972, and it has one of the lowest recidivism rates for juveniles in the nation.

Of course, these changes would only redress some of the injustices faced by children who encounter the juvenile justice system. To tackle the overall problem of juvenile crime, a well-informed citizenry will have to address its causes and build a response that truly meets the needs of all children.

Michele Magar is a Washington, D.C., journalist who covers civil rights.

13

The Female Fear

Margaret T. Gordon

In any large American city, "typical" rapes—conceived as a stranger attacking a lone woman in a dark, deserted place—are no longer news. Among the many rapes and attempted rapes that occur on a daily basis, only a small proportion are reported to the police. The police "unfound" a significant number of others—i.e., they find that the evidence does not support the charge—something that occurs with rape more frequently than with any other crime. Of those rapes that remain on the records, then, journalists pick out the more unusual, the more newsworthy, to report.

"Newsworthy" is the operative word here, for the unusual and the bizarre are key elements in defining what's news. But with rape, as with crime generally, the result is that readers and viewers get a diet of the atypical and unrepresentative. In fact, the media tend to report crimes in the reverse order of their frequency. Murder, for example, is the least frequently occurring crime in America, yet nearly half of the 5.6 violent crime stories printed daily in nine newspapers during a six-month period in three study cities—Philadelphia, Chicago and San Francisco— were about murders. Stories about rape and other sexual assaults, including those on children, appeared two to four times per week, depending on the newspaper.

The results of such coverage are predictable. Surveys show, for instance, that people believe about 25 percent of rape victims are murdered, and that the majority are so seriously hurt during their attacks that they have to be hospitalized. Police data show the percentage murdered is in fact closer to 3, and those hospitalized closer to 8 percent. (These data do not speak at all to the mental or emotional consequences of being sexually assaulted, or the numbers of victims suffering such damage.)

Among the things journalists do not report are *attempted* rapes, attacks when the victims escaped or at least avoided being raped. Police data here conflict with other sources: according to Uniform Crime Report (police) data, only one in four victims gets away, but Victimization Survey data (collected by the U.S. Census) indicate the opposite—that in every four attacks, three of the intended victims get away and one is raped. The Victimization Surveys are probably more accurate, inasmuch as women who have been attacked but escaped often don't bother to report the crime to the police. Newspaper portrayals, however, paint a very different picture: For every 14 news reports about rape, 13 are about completed rapes and one is about an attempted rape, often one with a bizarre angle. Since most women know only about the rapes the media report, the nature of the portrayals may explain why women believe both that most rapes are completed and that victims have very little chance of getting away.

The media's failure to report many attempted rapes also robs women of opportunities to learn about successful strategies with which to thwart attackers. For example, a story depicting the rape of a college student in the early evening hours may be truthful and accurate, yet women are likely to want to know many facts usually not included: What precipitated the attack? Exactly where was the woman before the attack? Did the woman fight back and, if so, were some strategies more effective than others? How frequent are such attacks in the neighborhood where it occurred? Where did the victim get help? Has the perpetrator been caught?

Surprisingly, the last question in particular most often goes unanswered by the media, leaving the impression that the perpetrator is still at large. The general absence of follow-up stories after the initial reports of rapes leaves readers and viewers ignorant of the subsequent fates of either perpetrator or victim and unable to gauge their own chances of being attacked.

Today, more than 65 percent of the women living in American cities are afraid to go out alone at night for fear of harm. This appalling statistic means that a significant portion of America's population is not really free.

The news media's coverage of rape seems even more salacious in the context of its other reporting. While increasing the amount of soft news and "infotainment" in newspapers and television in an effort to attract and keep suburban and youthful consumers, media executives also seem to hold on to their belief that violence and crime sell, and to insist that stories about sex crimes against women sell best.

When Rupert Murdoch bought the Chicago *Sun-Times* in 1983, many Chicagoans predicted that the tabloid would follow the strategy used by many of his other holdings and feature more violent crime and feature it more sensationally. Observers went on to predict that, in order to compete, the more staid, full-size *Chicago Tribune* would also print more crime stories and perhaps give them more sensational treatment.

The *Columbia Journalism Review*'s content analyses of the *Sun-Times* and *Tribune* for the year before and the two months following the Murdoch takeover support those predictions. That is, *both* papers increased their coverage of violent crimes, including rape. But the *Tribune* increased its crime coverage so much that the space devoted to rapes was nearly *double* what it had been before Murdoch's arrival in Chicago! When asked about their portrayals of sex crimes, media executives involved said, "We are just giving the public what it wants."

Are they? It is well known that the audiences for newspapers and television news have been dwindling for some time. Focus-group interviews with members of the reading and viewing public indicate people are losing confidence in the media and believe journalists are failing in their responsibilities. Yet analyses of the differences between the television fare during "sweeps weeks" and non-sweeps weeks make clear that media managers still believe large doses of sex, violence and sexual violence boost the ratings. They are also affected by what I refer to as the spectacular rape stories that seem to come along every few years involving bizarre circumstances or famous people—such as the pool table rape of a woman in New Bedford, Massachusetts, the recantation by a rape victim in Illinois several years after her alleged perpetrator had been imprisoned, and the William Kennedy Smith case.

The notoriety of the New Bedford case—the inspiration for the Academy Award-winning film *The Accused*—was heightened by the fact that the victim was alleged to have been gang-raped on a pool table while screaming for help from what was initially portrayed as a roomful of onlookers, none of whom came to her aid. Journalists converged on the town but did not bother to correct the impression given by earlier reports about large numbers of onlookers, despite the fact that further investigation indicated that in addition to the perpetrators only the bartender and a sleeping drunk were present. Reflective journalists admitted that the large number of bystander-witnesses made it a "better" story, more unusual, more bizarre. Once publicized, it was not in the interest of reporters to correct themselves.

Further, the very presence of the phalanx of journalists made the story into a bigger one. Their attendance at the trial, television cameras and all, and the eventual revelation of the name and face of the victim, caused other victims all over the country to drop their cases, lest they be treated the same way. This was also a concern raised by the Kennedy Smith case, when the alleged victim's name was printed in the *New York Times* and a Miami newspaper, and was subsequently used on national network news. The latter case also prompted discussion of the fairness of naming the accused if the accuser is not named: nearly every story about the case mentions the Kennedy name, which after all is what makes the story so newsworthy.

In the second case, years after the conviction of Gary Dotson on charges of rape, Cathleen Crowell Webb said a religious conversion caused her to admit that she had been lying and that Dotson should be freed. The media circus that followed included their appearing on talk shows together and being asked to shake hands for the viewers (which they did) and to hug (which they did not). The aftermath included not only soul-searching on the part of television journalists who exploited this story but accelerated concern from feminists that rape victims in general would be thought to be lying. After all, it had not been long since police in many jurisdictions had finally been persuaded not to administer lie detector tests to victims of rape. Legislators in Illinois were in the midst of revamping sexual assault laws, and this case and subsequent discussions of how to prevent women from falsely accusing men delayed passage of the new statutes for years.

Such bizarre and unusual stories mean, among other things, that the media give less time, attention and space to the day-to-day issues and concerns affecting the majority of women, to say nothing of the more typical rapes, attempted rapes, batterings and sexual harassment. They are also constant reminders to women of the danger they are in—and of how they might be treated by the media, should they be victimized.

My own research with colleague Stephanie Riger shows that nearly all women fear sexual assault at least some of the time, and about a third are "very afraid" most of the time. The latter take so many precautions that they make themselves virtual prisoners in their homes (undoubt-edly unaware that more rapes take place in or near victims' homes than any other place). Even the remaining two-thirds, who experience fear of sexual assault only twice a month or less—worrying more about di-vorce, losing their jobs or getting cancer—are periodically terrified of rape. The fear of sexual assault tends to become most acute when they learn about the rape of a friend or acquaintance, or read or hear about the rape of someone else. There are enough rapes daily in our nation's cities to produce a steady stream of these stories, and, based on intra-city comparisons, the women who read the newspapers containing the largest proportions of violent crime reports also indicate the highest lev-els of fear.

Not surprisingly, the response of many women to these circum-stances is not only fear, but also anger at a society that seems to refuse to take seriously crimes against women. I believe most women view rape as simply the far end of a continuum of assaults that also includes marital rape, attempted rape, spouse battering, sexual harassment and what some authors have labelled "mini rapes": whistles, pinches and other unwanted invasions.

History teaches women—and the news media support the lesson—that societal institutions have failed to take seriously these "trivia of women's everyday lives" since they do not act to reduce or eliminate them. Until recently, most of these issues have been taboo topics, and women have been expected to simply "deal with them" alone. When they do emerge from under the shrouds of secrecy, women victims have had difficulty "proving" the assaults or the impacts of those assaults to the satisfaction of others. Indeed, Anita Hill's charges of sexual harass-ment during the Clarence Thomas confirmation hearings were questioned in part because she had not sought help and had told only a few people at the time of the alleged assaults.

The spectacular implications of Hill's story, and the immense televi-sion and newspaper coverage accompanying the hearings, meant that a large percentage of the American population for the first time came to regard as important those issues of sexual harassment and their effects on women that have concerned feminists for years.

The relationship between media coverage of sexual assault and women's fear calls into question basic definitions of news, and the ad-equacy with which media currently fulfill their basic functions of informing and edifying the public. If the media are unable to portray reality in its proper context, it is likely people will continue to lose faith in the media and journalists' ability to "tell it like it is."

I believe the media's coverage of crime against women can and should shatter taboos, and—as in the Hill-Thomas hearings—bring issues before the public in a way that doesn't worsen the situation for women or for the media. All crimes against women should be appropriate topics for news stories, but the media should not exploit women or sensationalize these stories simply because they may be good for business. These stories should be handled in a way that doesn't further victimize the women involved, and without provoking more fear. I also believe that while the media cannot be held responsible for the impact of the portrayals they produce, they can do more to explain, contextualize and follow up their stories—and otherwise enable women to put them into perspective.

Perhaps a more important question is, "Is what's good for the news business necessarily good for society?" Commercial uses of crimes against women to increase ratings or circulation contribute to a climate of violence and fear and to the acceptance of urban violence and fear as simple facts of life. This state of affairs may be unintended, but it should not go unexamined. While the American public continues generally to support the U.S. Constitution, the erosion of public support for a free press worries journalists and scholars. Both constitutional referenda and social science research record an increasing belief that the media are abusing their protected freedoms and are making decisions about what to cover and how to cover it not with the public good in mind but what's best for their bottom lines. It is time to think again, to reconcile the impact of what they do with their First Amendment right to do it.

Margaret T. Gordon is dean of the Graduate School of Public Affairs at the University of Washington and a former senior fellow at The Freedom Forum Media Studies Center.

14

Firearms Follies: How the News
Media Cover Gun Control

Ted Gest

On October 16, 1991, George Hennard crashed his pickup truck into Luby's Cafeteria in Killeen, Texas, shot 23 customers to death for no apparent reason, and killed himself. News of the episode led that night's network newscasts and many of the next day's newspapers. As coincidence would have it, the mass murder occurred on the very day that the U.S. House of Representatives began floor debate on a wide-ranging crime bill. House members were to vote the next day on a proposal to ban the manufacture of certain so-called assault weapons.

After the "CBS Evening News" told the shooting story atop its October 16 broadcast, anchor Dan Rather turned to reporter Richard Threlkeld and asked, "Is Congress going to do anything to limit these assault weapons, and if so, what?" The reply: "We hope so." Threlkeld then told viewers about the coming House vote. The reporter's hope was not fulfilled; the House defeated the assault-gun measure. The media then took a predictable story line: Lobbying by the powerful National Rifle Association had overcome the shock of one of America's worst mass gun murders and stalled the latest attempt at gun control.

The episode hardly is remarkable in the annals of news coverage of guns. Actually, it is more or less par for the course. Most of the major media tied Killeen to the crime bill, although there was no evidence the proposal would have prevented Hennard from obtaining the guns he used in Luby's Cafeteria. The reasoning behind many reports was typically superficial, characterized by a *USA Today* editorial headlined, "Stop the madness; pass sane gun-control laws": "We have too few gun laws and too many guns.... Gun laws won't stop every killer. But they'll stop some. And the only way to save lives is one at a time."

America's news media consistently display a mixture of bias, carelessness and plain error in reporting issues involving guns. This indictment is not universal—scores of writers and editors have produced well-researched, fair stories, and gun control has not been singled out for poor reporting. But to varying degrees participants in the firearms debate concur that media coverage is poor. A spokesman for the National Rifle Association declares: "American news media are strongly biased against the NRA, prejudicial toward law-abiding gun owners, skeptical of the Second Amendment as a guarantor of an individual civil right, and critical of hunting, its cultural roots and its value in wildlife conservation." Handgun Control Inc., the leading lobby group favoring gun control, is far less critical, but a spokeswoman says the organization also has received a "bad deal" in some coverage that tends to treat the gun-control debate mostly as a political "David vs. Goliath" struggle and ignores the substance of what gun controls could accomplish. (Handgun Control once promoted the David-Goliath metaphor but has dropped it recently.) In the middle is the Treasury Department's Bureau of Alcohol, Tobacco and Firearms, which enforces the federal gun-control laws. Officials of ATF, too, fault the media for consistently inaccurate reporting on guns.

The prominence of firearms in the news seems inevitable. Crime is a prime subject of news coverage, and guns are a major means of committing crime. The FBI says that 64 percent of the nation's 20,045 murders in 1990 were committed with firearms, as well as 36 percent of the 639,271 reported robberies and 23 percent of the 1,054,863 reported aggravated assaults. Many of these offenses find their way into print or onto the airwaves, where the TV-news teaser line "film at 11" more often than not refers to some crime or disaster. The presumed public obsession with crime is not lost on politicians, who happily inflame the issue further. Against complex fiscal, ethnic and health problems, crime seems a simple issue, and easy to exploit; witness the prisoner-furlough ads that played a larger-than-deserved part in the 1988 presidential campaign. Into this controversial atmosphere enter the news media, which collectively are unsophisticated about reporting technical issues, whether they involve brain surgery, tactical nuclear weapons, environmental policy or firearms.

How do gun-control stories get on the front pages, nightly national newscasts and the covers of newsmagazines? In most cases, the reason is a dramatic incident such as the 1989 schoolyard killings in Stockton, California. In others, editors or producers simply decide that the gun-crime problem should be examined; hence the *Time* magazine cover story of July 17, 1989, that recounted the 464 killings in one week attributable to guns. The Cox newspaper chain has published long series on "Saturday Night specials" and assault weapons, and CBS and ABC have broadcast special programs on guns in recent years.

Considering coverage overall, the meager statistical evidence available indicates a tilt in favor of gun control. Rutgers University criminologist Tamryn Etten studied a sample of 117 newspaper stories in 1989 and concluded that 70 percent were "neutral or close to neutral," although the remaining 30 percent "were predominantly biased in the pro-control direction." A "media-monitoring service" commissioned by the National Rifle Association to review its press coverage counted 63,747 mentions of "NRA or its issues" from January 1989 through October 1991. The service evaluated 44.4 percent of the stories as unfavorable, 34.7 percent as favorable and 20.9 percent neutral.

Sins of commission and omission are all too common in stories about firearms. Among the major categories, escalating in significance:

• *Inexcusable factual errors and general ignorance.* Some errors are indeed inexcusable: Sarah Brady has been incorrectly identified as the founder of Handgun Control Inc.; a 1989 National Public Radio series suggested falsely that no constitutional expert would argue that the Second Amendment guarantees individuals the right to bear arms.

But more to the point, gun control—for all its prominence—is not considered an issue for which journalists require special training. Reporters in such fields as law, medicine, science, military and foreign affairs attend occasional briefings or seminars to learn fine points of their issues, but this rarely is true of firearms. Many new reporters do cover the police beat, but that is primarily to familiarize them with the local geography and the operations of their news organization in a setting where they can deal with relatively simple material. The human-interest elements of police stories usually take precedence over details such as what kind of gun an assailant may have used.

Examples of misreporting abound. Many media report that "assault weapons" are "high-powered." That sounds good, but it's incorrect.

Reporters and photographers were disappointed to learn after the Stockton episode that the type of gun used there would not even make a melon "explode" on camera. Many stories confuse automatic weapons like machine guns with semiautomatics that fire one shot for each trigger pull. There is also confusion about ammunition magazines. Many reports noted that the crime bill debated after Killeen would have limited gun clips to seven rounds, compared with the 17-round magazine used in Killeen. The stories generally failed to note that a competent gunman can change a clip in a second or two. Banning 17-round magazines may be a good idea, but it would do little to stem the gun-death toll.

Finally, the stylebooks that are supposed to help reporters and writers on technical matters are deficient when it comes to guns. The most prominent, published by the Associated Press, includes a section on "weapons" that does not discuss "assault weapons" but does provide such guidance as this definition of *automatic*: "a kind of pistol designed for automatic or semiautomatic firing. Its cartridges are held in a magazine" (with no explanation of *magazine*). How can a reporter make sense of that? A much better discussion can be found in the 1989 *Washington Post* "Deskbook on Style," which explains the difference between an automatic and a semiautomatic, as well as a magazine, and begins with the overall but oft-ignored instruction: "It is always a good idea to check the details about the caliber and firing mode of any firearm." It is also a good idea to check with police, the federal ATF or the NRA, any of which can demonstrate for reporters a firearm's capabilities.

Needless to say, ignorance results in misleading articles. Take the front-page *New York Times* story of October 18, 1991, headlined "House Resoundingly Defeats Ban on Semiautomatic Arms." The story said the bill would have banned "13 types of assault-like weapons." The article, like most others appearing that day, failed to note that seven of the 13 guns already had been banned for importation by ATF or had been redesigned since the bill was drafted so that they would not have been affected.

• *Editorial stands in news columns.* Major national print media such as the *New York Times*, the *Washington Post* and many influential regional newspapers disproportionately favor gun control on their editorial pages. It is difficult to prove that such editorializing colors news coverage, but *Time* magazine has crossed the line. The weekly answered complaints from readers about its 1989 cover story on murders with a forthright admission that its editors were attempting "to keep the gun-availability issue resolutely in view. Such an editorial closing of ranks represents the exception rather than the rule in the history of the magazine.... the time for opinions on the dangers of gun availability is long since gone.... our appeal is for consideration of reasonable control over gun ownership." Says Robert Lichter of the Washington-based Center for Media & Public Affairs, "It pops your eyes open that the magazine is so certain of itself that it takes for granted that there is no obligation to be balanced; they believe it's obvious that we have to get rid of guns."

• *Bias.* Most journalists attempt to keep personal opinions out of their work, but critics charge that a disproportionate number of journalists have an antipathy toward guns because they grew up in big-city households where guns were uncommon—what sociologist William Tonso of the University of Evansville calls a "cosmopolitan" bias. A 1985 *Los Angeles Times* survey of journalists' personal opinions showed that 78 percent favor "stricter controls on private ownership of handguns," compared with 50 percent of readers of the newspapers surveyed. Evidence of overt bias is scattered, but most anecdotes have an anti-NRA flavor. The NRA charges that when one gun-control organization held a press conference, a few journalists sported the group's promotional buttons. *Time* writer Strobe Talbott declared on a televised talk show that the NRA "is nothing less than an American disgrace, and it's really great to see them take one on the chin." NBC anchor Garrick Utley said that what "Thomas Paine described...simply as 'Common Sense'...pretty well describes the case for gun control today."

• *Omitting crucial information.* Some stories seem bent on creating trends even if the facts do not support the thesis. Criminologist Gary Kleck of Florida State University recalls being interviewed by *USA Today* in June 1989 after five Florida children had been injured in gun accidents in a week. Kleck stressed federal data showing that fatal gun accidents involving children under 10 had dropped from 227 in 1974 to 92 in 1987, but the resulting story ignored that fact and instead implied that such incidents were on the rise.

• *Questionable news judgment.* The prominence given by major media to gun control seems to proceed from the dubious assumption that control likely would have a significant impact on crime. Consider the Brady waiting-period bill pending in Congress. After the House approved it last May, the *Washington Post* said in a lead story that the vote gave "momentum to the most far-reaching gun-control measure to pass the

House in more than two decades." The article called the action a "stinging defeat for the NRA and a major victory for gun-control advocates and the Bradys...." A front-page story in the *New York Times* reported proponents' "beating back a vigorous challenge by opponents of gun control who said the measure would punish law-abiding gunowners." The *Wall Street Journal* said the vote underscored that "concern about the country's rising murder rate has eroded the influence of the pro-gun lobby led by the National Rifle Association."

Coverage of assault weapons also raises questions of news judgment. A 1985 *Newsweek* cover story estimated (with little evidence) that there were 500,000 "military-style assault guns" in the nation. Police officers began to report more crimes committed with semiautomatic weapons, and a group called the Educational Fund to End Handgun Violence asserted in 1988 that "the sale and misuse of assault weapons has escalated dramatically during the 1980s." The Stockton schoolyard shooting of January 17, 1989, put the story on front pages and network newscasts, and ever since the media have been full of stories and editorials about plans to restrict or ban the weapons.

Putting aside the question of exactly what an assault weapon is, how prevalent are they? The data are inconclusive at best. In an editorial in October 1991, on the eve of the House crime debate, the *New York Times* stated: "Federal agents find that assault weapons account for less than 1 percent of all privately owned guns but more than 10 percent of guns involved in crimes." The same day, a *Washington Post* editorial said: "Though the weapons represent only one-half of 1 percent of all private guns in the country, [Representative Charles Schumer, D-N.Y.] says they are used in 1 out of 10 crimes."

But the widely reported "10 percent" figure is unverified. It stems from a 1989 investigative series by the Cox newspaper chain concluding that assault guns "were used in one of every 10 crimes that resulted in a firearms trace last year." The last part of that key sentence conveniently disappears from most references. "Traces" are not equivalent to crimes. In the 15-month period in question, the federal ATF bureau was asked 42,758 times by other law-enforcement agencies to trace guns used in crimes. But nearly 500,000 violent crimes each year are committed with guns. No one knows how the trace requests relate to those 500,000 crimes, but experts say that assault weapons are probably used in fewer than one of 10 crimes.

This is not the only erroneous notion that has been used to justify extensive press coverage of a gun-control issue. Maryland's 1988 referendum on a plan to ban certain "Saturday Night specials" received much national attention based on the oft-stated assumption that it would have been the first such ban in the nation. Yet four other states already had imposed such a prohibition.

• *Interest-group tactics*. Handgun Control Inc. is more aggressive than the NRA at getting its story out. HCI frequently faxes and mails material to reporters on the latest congressional or state gun-control fight. NRA officials charge that their views have been represented inadequately in articles and broadcasts, but the group often makes it difficult for reporters to obtain those views. The NRA never has seen fit to put this writer on a mailing list even though he has been the principal reporter covering guns for more than a decade for a national newsmagazine that reaches 12 million readers a week. The group usually answers telephone calls, although it essentially stonewalled a request for interviews several years ago for a story on one of its periodic internal fights. (After several calls, the NRA provided a small boxful of background material for this article.)

• *Personality journalism*. Sarah Brady has emerged as the leading figure in the gun-control movement, as exemplified by a cover story about her in the *New York Times Magazine*. Hers seems a compelling story: A top White House official is seriously wounded in an attack on the President, and his spouse (later joined by the ex-official himself, in a wheelchair) becomes a prominent gun-control advocate.

By contrast, the major media have showed little interest in the story of how J. Warren Cassidy went from being an insurance salesman to leader of the NRA. Cassidy has since left the organization, but a few years ago he described in an interview how he became active in the pro-gun movement. Long a hunter and NRA member, it was only after a Massachusetts sheriff led a drive to put a handgun ban on a state ballot in 1976 that Cassidy, then mayor of Lynn, Massachusetts, was drafted to be a spokesperson for opponents. Cassidy says he went to the *Boston Globe* editorial page to make his case and was told, "We're not reporting on this campaign. We're against you. We will print no letters to the editor on your side of the issue." And, Cassidy recalls, "They did not."

The NRA has published advertisements in which members tell why they use guns, but the organization has not played the personality game as well as has Handgun Control. In fact, the NRA has shunned that tactic to its disadvantage. Last spring when the CBS program "48 Hours" told the behind-the-scenes story of lobbying over the Brady bill, gun-control forces allowed CBS cameras to follow them around for two days. The NRA refused.

Contributing to the NRA's wobbly public image is the media tendency to play up the theme of whether the organization is gaining or waning. A *USA Today* story last spring about the House's passage of the Brady bill alluded to a quote from Representative Charles Schumer, chairman of the House Subcommittee on Crime, in a headline reporting, "Stranglehold of NRA now broken." It is true that a waiting period may be enacted this year after a long battle, but the NRA's death has been greatly exaggerated. When the assault-weapon ban was handily defeated in the House last fall, for example, media reported the result as "surprising," even though the NRA has consistently prevailed on this issue. Meanwhile, notes the Bureau of Alcohol, Tobacco and Firearms, the media have overlooked a major change the NRA helped write into the McClure-Volkmer gun bill passed by Congress in 1986 that effectively allows convicted felons in most states to regain their right to obtain firearms once their "civil rights" are restored, usually as soon as they leave prison, probation or parole. One can debate the merits of the provision, but it would undermine one of the prime concepts behind the Brady waiting-period measure.

Then there are cheap shots like a 1990 column by Jim Schutze in the *Dallas Times Herald* repeatedly calling the NRA "the pro-murder lobby," and the erroneous reference by *Washington Post* television critic Tom Shales to Charlton Heston as the "hired shill for the NRA in their execrable commercials" on gun control. (Heston says he sought no payment.) Or the Cox chain—one of the more enterprising on firearms—publishing a story on Sarah Brady and NRA lobbyist Jim Baker with a headline calling Baker "Mr. Fire" and Brady "Mrs. Nice."

Finally, the media stand accused of handling interest-group advertisements erratically, too. The NRA complains that CBS and other media reject some of its ads as too political. Handgun Control counters that media use erroneous NRA ads too readily, such as one accusing gun-control backer and then-San Jose Police Chief Joseph McNamara of having favored legalizing marijuana and another charging that a bill by Senator Howard Metzenbaum would have forced 30 million Americans to "give up" semiautomatic guns.

The sustained news coverage of gun control undoubtedly has some impact on public policy, but is difficult to pinpoint. After the 1989 Stockton killings, the Bush administration banned the import of certain foreign-made assault weapons, and a few states and localities have enacted assault-gun bans. Several major police organizations have supported the actions, saying that their officers have been targets of such weapons. ATF says it was preparing the foreign assault-weapon ban before Stockton, although officials admit that the torrent of news coverage helped create an atmosphere in which the White House could approve the ban over the objections of pro-gun groups.

News organizations and interest groups could follow up more on the implications and impact of all widely publicized gun-control measures. Most media have not explored in depth such questions as: How can the Bush administration reconcile its support of a ban on foreign-made weapons with its opposition to a ban on domestically manufactured ones? How is the ban being undermined by approval of 100,000 permits for reconfigured versions of the banned weapons? Such examinations would shed more light on the public debate when episodes like Stockton and Killeen produce demands for reform.

Some have written such follow-ups, but they usually get short shrift. Last spring, the *New York Times* reported on page 12 that as Congress considered the Brady bill, "Questions are being raised about how effective even stricter measures have been in California." The *Times* reported a month later that Virginia's system of instant background checks of handgun buyers "underscores the limits of any effort to determine who is fit to own a firearm." An April 14, 1991, story in the *Philadelphia Inquirer* said, "On the day Ronald Reagan gave up his longstanding opposition to a federal handgun-control bill, Jean-Claude Pierre Hill walked out of a rural Virginia gun shop with two newly purchased $529 Colt .45 semiautomatic pistols." Hill, a psychiatry student at Philadelphia's Hahnemann University Hospital, was later charged with shooting a 48-year-old businessman and two of his companions in an apparently unprovoked street assault. By not disclosing that he had been found by a court to be a danger to himself and others, Hill evaded the record-checking system's aim of denying handguns to those with records of severe mental illness.

Gun control is one of the most emotional issues of our times, and more common ground might be reached if the news media tried harder to get the facts straight amid all the blood and gore.

Ted Gest is senior editor/legal affairs at U.S. News & World Report. *A version of this article was presented at the 1991 annual meeting of the American Society of Criminology.*

15

Desperadoes and Lawmen: The Folk Hero

Richard Maxwell Brown

Consider the life of a certain American of the late-19th and early 20th centuries: He was born in 1848; rose to ample prosperity in the far West; married a mercantile heiress in an unbroken union of five decades; hobnobbed with governors, senators, millionaires and movie stars; was idolized by the youthful minister who went on to found America's most exclusive private school; spent his last years in southern California; was a lifelong, conservative member of the Republican Party; and at his death in 1929 had his funeral sermon preached by the pastor of the fashionable Wilshire Congregational Church of Los Angeles.

This was Wyatt Earp. These facts of his life contradict the myth that swirled out of the gunsmoke of the famous 1881 fight near the O.K. Corral in Tombstone, Arizona, when Earp led two of his brothers and Doc Holliday in their conquest of Billy Clanton and the McLaury brothers, the three outlaws who opposed them.

In fact Wyatt Earp's role in the Tombstone shootout is of a piece with his standing as a conservative Westerner. The two sides in the gunfight near the O.K. Corral represented antagonistic social forces aligned against one another time and again in what I call the Western Civil War of Incorporation, which raged throughout the American West from the 1850s to the 1920s. On one side of that war—whose venues were the gun battles, riots and lynchings of the cattle ranges, mining camps, mill towns, logging shows, wheat fields and urban metropolises of the West—was the conservative consolidating authority of capital spearheaded by the corporate forces of industry, finance, business and land enclosure. On the other side were the dissident—often outlaw—forces of violent resistance to the trend that was, in the 1982 conception of Yale scholar Alan Trachtenberg, incorporating all of America, not just the West, into a society dominated by the conservative forces of property. Many of the outlaws who resisted the incorporating trend embodied traditional social values in which bonds of kin and custom were held more dearly than the more modern principles of law and order espoused by the incorporators of the West.

Because so much writing on the "Wild West" has been meretricious, serious historians of the West have until recently avoided, as though an intellectual plague, the entire subject of outlaws and gunfighters. In so doing they largely turned their backs on a prolific and violent conflict that offers a historical interpretation linking outlaws and gunfighters to the mainstream of Western history. What has flourished in place of such an interpretation is a contradictory folklore of Western heroism, a narrative told first in newspapers, magazines and dime novels, and later by Hollywood, that reveals Americans' deep ambiguity about crime and justice.

The gunfight near the O.K. Corral was merely the high point in a local chapter of the Western Civil War of Incorporation: Arizona's Cochise County War of 1881–1882. Tombstone, the seat of huge Cochise County, was surrounded by rural range country that was dominated by a faction of cowboy outlaws, most of them Southern or Texan in origin, Democratic in politics, of Confederate sympathy in regard to the war that had ended 15 years before, and engaged in the crime of cattle rustling. On the other hand, the boomtown of Tombstone was dominated by Republican industrialists and business and professional men who feared that the lawlessness of the cowboy-outlaw faction would discourage crucial Eastern and Californian investment in Tombstone's mines.

Thus was the incorporating clique of Cochise County entrenched in the urban center of Tombstone, and heading the town's incorporating faction of Republican Party nabobs was its greatest mining magnate, Dartmouth graduate E.B. Gage; former Rutgers football player John P. Clum, who was both mayor and editor of the *Tombstone Epitaph,* the town's GOP mouthpiece; George W. Parsons, an ambitious banker; and magistrate Wells Spicer, who would eventually find the Earps and Holliday without fault in their slaying of the three cowboys. Also in this group (although too young and new in town to be a leader) and idolizing Wyatt Earp was the Massachusetts aristocrat Endicott Peabody, in Tombstone to establish the local Episcopal church before going back East to found the elite Groton School, become Franklin D. Roosevelt's head-master, and, much later, lead the private devotions of the Roosevelt family at FDR's first and second presidential inaugurations.

The Earps themselves were not just law enforcers in Tombstone and Cochise County but—true to their social colors and political prefer-ences—enthusiastic and successful speculators and investors in Tomb-stone real estate and mining properties. As the leader of the Earp brothers, Wyatt's courage, gunfighting talent and social conservatism attracted Gage, Clum and the rest, who turned to Wyatt and his like-minded, like-skilled brothers to curb the unruly cowboy-outlaw faction they feared and detested. After the Earps and Holliday gunned down Clanton and the McLaurys near the O.K. Corral, Wyatt—brandishing a U.S. deputy marshal's commission gained through his Republican political connec-tions—conducted a whirlwind campaign of killing that shattered Cochise County's anti-incorporating cowboy-outlaw faction.

The 33-year-old Wyatt Earp had come a long way from his early days as an obscure Great Plains rounder given to horse theft, confidence games and bunco artistry. Earp had first begun to change his reputation for the better by serving as an able lawman in Dodge City, Kansas, before go-ing on to Tombstone, and in Arizona he settled down to the strong iden-tity of conservative Republican, which put in the shade the misdeeds of his often ne'er-do-well youth.

Although it was his skill as a gunfighter that made him a historically significant American of his time, the one word—with all its implica-tions—that best describes Wyatt Earp is "Republican," for it was as an incorporation gunfighter that Wyatt Earp served the conservative GOP in the West.

But this social and biographical reality has been eclipsed by the myth of Wyatt Earp and the gunfight near the O.K. Corral, a powerful image that really began with the publication of two early 20th-century books that were long on myth and short on reality: Walter Noble Burns' *Tomb-stone: An Iliad of the Southwest* (1929) and the appealing but highly spurious biography by journalist and free-lancer Stuart N. Lake, *Wyatt Earp: Frontier Marshal* (1931). Earp walked as a living legend for nearly 50 years after his Tombstone exploits, and despite the backlash of some vociferous anti-Burns and anti-Lake writings, the popular persona of Wyatt Earp was later fixed by a widely viewed television series and by the classic films *My Darling Clementine* (1946) and *Gunfight at the*

O.K. Corral (1957). The myth of Wyatt Earp in the public mind has a long lead on more realistic appraisals, defeated by the legend of the heroic gunfighter and the long absence of any serious scholarly effort to find out what really happened in the conflict between outlaws and lawmen in the Old West.

The dissidents who resisted the conservative trend of Western incorporation were a varied lot. Many were law-abiding opponents of incorporation who expressed their opposition through the ballot box, sometimes as Democrats, often by way of more radical third parties such as the Populists. More actively opposed to oppressive corporate industrialism of the West, and often more violent, were the rising labor unions (including the "Wobblies," the Industrial Workers of the World) and insurgent farmers. In the southern Central Valley of California of the 1870s and '80s, for example, pioneers, energized by the homestead ethic, fought a losing battle against eviction in a violent land dispute with the millionaire owners of the Southern Pacific Railroad: Leland Stanford, Collis P. Huntington and Charles Crocker. The railroad claimed the farmer-occupied land on the basis of a huge but controversial federal land grant, and eventually the railroad magnates' allies in the federal judiciary upheld the Southern Pacific's dispossession of the small farmers.

Among the other consolidating powers in the war of incorporation were such regionally and nationally famous figures as Californian Stephen J. Field, the conservative pillar of the U.S. Supreme Court, who sat concurrently on the federal circuit bench in the Golden State; the cattle kings of New Mexico, Wyoming, Montana and elsewhere; top industrialists in mining and transportation; powerful figures in business, finance and law; and the governors and senators (most of them Republicans) who represented all in politics and government.

The bastions of the incorporating faction—banks, railroads, and ranching and railroad land enclosers—were natural targets for those unbowed dissidents on the far fringes of the Western Civil War of Incorporation, the outlaw gangs. There were many such gangs, but the most notable included the one headed by Jesse James, which flourished by robbing banks and railroads in Missouri and surrounding states from 1866 to 1881, and the smaller, shorter-lived but deadly range-country band of Billy the Kid.

The career of Billy the Kid, perhaps more than any other, illustrates both the reality behind the Western outlaw myth and the myth's enduring popularity. Emerging by 1878—at 18 years of age—as the top gun-fighter of vast Lincoln County, New Mexico, William Bonney had tried to find a law-abiding niche as a cowboy but instead found himself a fugitive when the territory's Republican governor, General Lew Wallace (soon to be the famous author of *Ben-Hur*), reneged on his promise to pardon the Kid for a killing. Turning to cattle theft in the Texas Pan-handle and Lincoln County, Billy and his gang soon antagonized the county's chief incorporators, the legendary cattle baron John Chisum and the rising mercantile entrepreneur Joseph C. Lea of Roswell. To-gether Chisum and Lea boosted gunfighter Pat Garrett into the office of county sheriff, and Garrett did his job. He broke up the Kid's gang and shot to death his erstwhile friend Billy in July 1881.

The myth of Billy the Kid began to take hold in the last year of his life, first told in newspapers and 10-cent books that portrayed the Kid as a mad-dog killer. Soon Garrett provided his own version, much of it ghost-written for him by journalist and friend Ash Upson, published in 1882. The book was rife with Upson's wild fantasies for the Kid's early life, but Garrett's conclusion accurately stated the social significance of the outlaw's short career. With the death of the Kid, wrote Garrett (or Upson for him but in sentiments true to Garrett), "Lincoln County now enjoys a season of peace and prosperity" with "no desperadoes...to scare out citizens from their labors, or disturb their slumbers. Stock wanders over the ranges in security, and vast fields of waving grain greet the eye...." In other words, Lincoln County had been forcefully incorporated in the interest of the leading stock raisers and merchants of the region. It was all this that made the slayer of Billy the Kid a hero to Theodore Roosevelt, who, 20 years later as president, rewarded Garrett with a coveted appointment as U.S. Collector of Customs in El Paso.

The historical reality of Billy the Kid as a resister gunfighter in the Western Civil War of Incorporation has been overwhelmed by the mighty myth of Billy the Kid as a classic "social bandit"—an image graphically alive today in the popular films *Young Guns* and *Young Guns II*. The "social bandit," according to a formulation conceived by British histo-rian E.J. Hobsbawm, is one whose outlaw deeds enjoy widespread ap-proval in society. The image is abundant in European and North American history, going back to the medieval prototype of Robin Hood. Billy the Kid in real life had strong support among the anti-incorporating Anglo cowboys and small ranchers of Lincoln County, as well as the Hispanic villagers of the area. A local folklore depicting Billy the Kid as a hero was codified in Walter Noble Burns' captivating but undependable book *The Saga of Billy the Kid* (1926). Since Burns, there has been an avalanche of mythic treatments of Billy the Kid in film and fiction, ranging from Aaron Copland's *Billy the Kid* ballet (1938) to the current Hollywood interpretation in the *Young Guns* movies.

The anti-myth of Billy the Kid as a psychopathic killer has gained currency in recent decades, but it has yet to match or overcome the Kid's image as a social bandit, nor is it based on reality. Of sunny good nature, the Kid was a lethal gunfighter but no psychopath. His real toll of human life was less than half of the 21 kills—one for each of the 21 years of his life—that the mythic Billy the Kid supposedly notched into his gun belt. A century after he died, the Kid's bibliographic file contained thousands of items of all kinds, but not until 1989 did there appear the first and, so far, only historically respectable biography, that by Robert M. Utley.

Although by 1920 the incorporating forces in the war of incorporation had won a great victory in routing their opponents—from Jesse James and Billy the Kid to the Wobblies who fought them after 1900—the ironic outcome in the realm of myth and ideology was to a considerable extent a victory for the defeated faction of gunfighting outlaws, who often came to enjoy heroic status as social bandits.

Yet the winning side in the Western Civil War of Incorporation generated its own mythic heroes—not just Wyatt Earp and Pat Garrett, but the prototypical Western gunfighter and officer of the law, Wild Bill Hickok. In a nationally televised speech in 1953, President Dwight Eisenhower paid tribute to this Abilene, Kansas, hometown hero, whom he evoked in a metaphor when he said if, like Wild Bill, you could meet your opponent "face to face and took the same risks as he did, you could get away with almost anything, as long as the bullet was in front."

Wild Bill Hickok was no phony. He was a paragon of gunplay, a highly effective frontier marshal in Kansas, and one whose bravery and skill were deeply admired by George Armstrong Custer, who knew him well. Hickok, like Wyatt Earp from a Civil War-era family of Midwestern unionists, was also like Earp and Garrett an incorporation gunfighter. He enforced the law against the tough Texan cowboys whose violence in Kansas cow towns like Abilene and Dodge City jeopardized the profits of the Northern, Republican businessmen who dominated such communities. Hickok was himself an ardent Republican, whose abolitionist father had operated a stop on the Underground Railroad in Illinois. Wild Bill had honed his marksman's eye during the Civil War by fighting as a scout in the Union Army in Missouri and Arkansas, the same territory covered by rebel raider "Bloody Bill" Anderson, whose followers included Jesse and Frank James, Cole and Jim Younger.

It may have been an early gunfighting exploit of Wild Bill Hickok that inspired the most influential and emulated scene in formula-Western fiction—the showdown, in which two opposing gunfighters stride down the main street of a Western town ready to draw and fire. Hickok's July 1865 killing of ex-Confederate scout Dave Tutt in the public square of Springfield, Missouri, was given national notoriety by a highly colored profile of wild Bill in *Harper's*, America's favorite magazine of the era. According to historian Kent Ladd Steckmesser, the event may have inspired the famous showdown etched by Philadelphia aristocrat Owen Wister in the climactic pages of his 1902 novel *The Virginian*. Wister's showdown pitted the villain, Trampas, against a heroic local cowboy known as the Virginian, whose betrothed nervously awaited the outcome of the fight in her hotel room. As the sunset glowed over the Wyoming mountains to the west, Trampas fired first, but the hero's flawless aim left the villain dying in the dust. Following marriage the next day, hero and sweetheart rode away to their honeymoon in the mountains.

No single item had a greater impact on the popular mythology of outlaw and gunfighter in print and film than *The Virginian*, but few readers recognize the secondary plot that lurks behind the romantic one. The book is a fictional but realistic portrayal of the 1892 Johnson County War in Wyoming, a key episode in the Western Civil War of Incorporation that pitted land-monopolizing ranch kings (who were often arrogant Eastern and British aristocrats) against an array of small ranchers, homesteaders and cattle rustlers. Politically the grandees were mostly Republicans, and they had the powerful backing of party politicos in Wyoming and Washington, including then-President Benjamin Harrison, while the resisters were Democrats and Populists. Wister, an ultra-conservative Republican who loved Wyoming, had good friends among the cattle-baron incorporators of Wyoming, and his fictional version of the Johnson County War was *their* version.

Wister dedicated his book to his friend President Theodore Roosevelt, who as a young cattle king in North Dakota and Montana had been a would-be anti-rustler vigilante. Roosevelt loved the book and no doubt admired its ideological plot about the Johnson County War. But like millions, Roosevelt was even more attracted to the other, romantic plot of the odious villain, the gunfighting hero and his sweetheart, the symbol of civilized society in the West to which the Virginian dedicates his gunfire.

Aside from the literary quality of popular Western fiction, critics have focused on the values it upholds—the meaning of its mythology. A persuasive scholarly view holds that popular Western fiction, whether in print or film, embodies a deep formula in which the hero mediates between civilization and savagery (or, in similar terms, between culture and nature or order and chaos). In this deep formula the gunfighting hero (like the Virginian) is a transitional figure, one who reluctantly employs the violence of the frontier West to establish the peaceable society of civilized values that is meant to succeed the chaotic, and often evil, pioneer phase.

The reality of the Western Civil War of Incorporation produced a conflict, indeed a kind of cognitive split, in the mythology of the Western outlaw and gunfighter. The winning side in the Western Civil War of Incorporation bred a socially conservative myth of the hero—for example, the fictional Virginian and the real Wild Bill Hickok and Wyatt Earp. The losing side generated a dissident social-bandit myth in which the heroes were outlaws like Billy the Kid, Jesse James, Butch Cassidy, and banditos Joaquin Murieta of California and Gregorio Cortez of Texas. The socially conservative myth has, on the whole, been dominant (but not by much)—probably because it engages fear of chaos against the security of order. Yet many Americans have been strongly attracted to the losers' version of the Western Civil War of Incorporation. Michael Cimino's flawed but powerful film *Heaven's Gate* (1980) was, *contra* Wister, a social-bandit interpretation of the Johnson County War. Ironically, one influential writer, Walter Noble Burns, contributed to both mythologies: to the socially conservative myth with his treatment of Wyatt Earp and to the social-bandit image with his book on Billy the Kid.

Indeed, both the conservative mythic hero and the dissident social bandit appeal equally to a great many Americans. These competing versions of the Western myth endure because they reflect a deep ambivalence in the American mind about established power and dissident protest.

Richard Maxwell Brown is Beekman Professor of Northwest and Pacific History at the University of Oregon and president of the Western History Association.

16

Making a Killing:
An Interview with Elmore Leonard

Craig L. LaMay

Elmore Leonard is the reigning patriarch of American crime fiction, the author of 29 novels and owner of a prose style and narrative skill that have drawn wide acclaim. Seemingly the heir to Raymond Chandler and Dashiell Hammett, Leonard drew his own inspiration elsewhere: from writers as varied as Ernest Hemingway and Richard Bissell, and the great crime films of the 1930s and '40s. Employing a reporter's ear and a gift for interior monologue that makes even the most cutthroat villains seem...familiar, Leonard's work reaches beyond mere genre writing.

Leonard himself is famously reluctant to discuss his work in such terms, seeing himself instead as a journeyman in his chosen field—at most, perhaps, a successful entertainer. Writing in the *Village Voice* in 1982, Ken Tucker said, "Elmore Leonard strikes me as being the finest thriller writer alive, primarily because he does his best to efface style, and has done this so successfully that few readers know about him at all."

Leonard did work long and hard for his success: He began his career as an advertising copywriter, penning westerns on the side, then screenplays. One of his westerns, *Hombre,* is now considered a small classic, and it is the only one of his many books that, in his view, Hollywood hasn't made a mess of. The $10,000 rights fee he earned from the sale of Hombre in 1965 convinced him to rethink his writing career. He made the jump to a new market—crime fiction—producing what many consider some of his finest books—*52 Pickup, The Switch, Split Images, Touch*—in the late 1960s and '70s. In 1983, with the publication of

LaBrava, his 23rd book, Leonard was "discovered," according to a *New York Times* headline at the time, and two years later, *Glitz* brought him his first major financial success and landed him on the cover of *Newsweek,* a 61-year-old overnight sensation. Since then he has followed with a series of best-sellers, most recently *Maximum Bob.* His 30th novel, *Rum Punch,* will be published by Delacorte/Dell next summer.

You are well known for the preparation you do in advance of writing. Do you use your research to construct your characters or to fill in the narrative, or both?

Elmore Leonard: The research is very specific, and for the most part it has to do with plot. For *Maximum Bob* I had already met officers with the Palm Beach County Sheriff's office, and the judge was a friend of mine. I wanted to use a probation officer—to see the crime or crimes from the probation officer's point of view—rather than a law enforcement officer. So my researcher started looking at judges who were in trouble and probation officers in their particular jurisdictions, so I could decide who was going to do what. But for the most part my characters aren't based on anybody. The research is for the purpose of plotting.

Reviewers often comment on what one called your "Panasonic ear"— an ability to render dialogue that sounds real and not written, to capture conversations almost verbatim and with all their nuances. J. Anthony Lukas, who should know about these things, has said you are "very much the reporter." Have you ever worked as a journalist, anywhere?

Leonard: No, though I did a piece for the *Detroit News Sunday Magazine* in 1978. I was introduced to a homicide squad, and I hung out with them. It was the kind of job where a professional reporter would spend two or three days following them around and then a day or so writing it, and then that would be it. I didn't write a word until I was with them for three weeks. I didn't know what to do—I didn't even know what tense to use—and finally decided that I could do it in my own style, that I could tell a lot of it in dialogue that would get their sound. At least they would swear that it was their sound.

Did you enjoy the job?

Leonard: Yeah. I went back after I had written the piece because I realized this was a gold mine. Squad Seven at that time, they were the hotshots. They were assigned to tougher homicides—not the floaters or the mom-and-pop things, but homicides that were committed in association with a felony. A lot of the material I got there went into *City Primeval.*

Do you ever get ideas for your characters from straight-up crime reporting?

Leonard: Yeah. I was at some kind of a seminar in Key West about four years ago. Carl Hiaasen came up to me and he mentioned the book— I think the book was either *LaBrava* or *Stick*—and he said, "Did you get some of your background stuff, some of your research out of stories that were in *Tropic*?" the *Miami Herald* Sunday magazine. I said yes, I did. He said, "I wrote those." I said, "Thank you, good stuff."

Many newspeople say that crime news is really just a kind of weird form of entertainment, where the highest standard is that of a "good story well told." What do you give a reader in fiction that he doesn't get from a journalism feature story?

Leonard: I want my characters in my stories to sound as though they *did* come out of the paper—not in the style, but certainly in content. In *Maximum Bob,* for example, two different reviewers in Detroit looked at it. One of them reviews a lot of crime and mystery stories. He reads *Maximum Bob* and says, "It fails because there's no redemption in it." I had no intention of having any of my characters redeem themselves, because it's not realistic. The other review of the book, in the *Detroit News,* by a judge, said you never know who's going to make it to the end of one of my stories, and that if I keep doing it this way, you might have to look for my books in the nonfiction section of the store. So it's coming out of newspapers.

Do you have a favorite reporter whose work you follow?

Leonard: No, not really. I am fascinated by what at one time was called the new journalism, where whatever happens to the reporter becomes part of the story. You can learn from so many different kinds of writing. I know I can learn from other novels. I'm always reading that way, and after 40 years I'm still learning, still trying to make it better.

You've said many times that you weren't influenced by the old school of crime fiction as represented by Dashiell Hammett and Raymond Chandler.

Leonard: No, not at all, because I didn't come out of that tradition, which to me is unrealistic. That particular kind of fiction, that particular kind of world and that way of talking, I think, was made up. That was not based necessarily on the way it was, and then hundreds and hundreds of writers have followed that first-person, private-eye way of writing, full of imagery.

Their private eyes were more traditional heroes, and you don't go in for traditional heroes?

Leonard: First of all, I couldn't imagine a private eye as a hero. I've seen the kind of boring work they do. I could write a private-eye story. Maybe I will sometime.

Let's talk about television. You've been quoted as saying that you didn't like "Hill Street Blues" or "Miami Vice." But I've read elsewhere that you thought that "Barney Miller," a sitcom, was the most realistic cop show on TV. Why is that?

Leonard: Yeah. I thought "Barney Miller" was the way it is in a squad room. I liked "Miami Vice" when it first started, and I liked some of "Hill Street Blues." What amazed me was all the activity in the station house in "Hill Street Blues." It was as though there was an earthquake outside: people running around, crowded. If you go into the police head-quarters in downtown Detroit—at 1300 Beauvien—there's nothing going on. You see a couple of guys sitting watching television on a snowy screen. There's very little going on, and this is a high-murder-rate city, with all kinds of crime.

"Barney Miller" was so realistic to me, like squad rooms that I've seen. Good humor, too. None of it was ever that funny, except that those actors were so good. The timing was so good. It made it very, very funny. I've seen cops the same way; they all have that kind of a dry, laconic sense of humor.

A couple of years ago you were slated to write a TV series for MGM, weren't you, based in New Orleans?

Leonard: I did a cop show set in New Orleans called "Wilder."

What happened to it?

Leonard: Beats me. I think it was probably too realistic for the studio. It wasn't theatrical enough, not gimmicky enough.

You're well known for your reluctance to take yourself too seriously, or even to let other people take you too seriously. At the same time, you're pretty well established as a notable American fiction writer. Your name pops up in the New York Review of Books, *the* London Review of Books *and other places. When Delacorte-Dell signed you in '89, Carole Baron, the president, declared that you were "bigger than that" when someone suggested you were just a genre writer. At least one scholar has attributed this kind of attention to what he calls your gift as an Ameri-can "social historian." What do you make of all that? Is what you do just entertainment, or is there more to it than that?*

Leonard: No, there's not more to it. It's like an interviewer asking me about "themes" and about getting deeper into the story and intentions, why I do it and all. To me, writing stories sounded like a pretty good idea, if you could get away with it. If you could develop a way of writing, if you could think up some good stories, make enough money to live on, that would be wonderful. But you find out that there aren't that many people who can live off writing. Maybe if you really apply yourself and work hard, you can do it. I did. I got up at 5 o'clock in the morning back in the '50s to do it. So it's working out. But the purpose is to do it, to entertain myself, to satisfy myself in the doing of it, not in the making of the money, not in the getting any kind of notoriety. That gets in the way more than it does anything else.

Several years ago, when discussing your characters, you said in a New York Times Magazine *article that you "don't try to go into the psychology of the guy's makeup. That doesn't interest me, and I don't think it interests the reader." At the same time, of course, you're known as a master of character. It almost seems that you don't even worry about your characters' state of mind because once you create these people they aren't yours anymore. They just take off into the narrative and do what they will. Is that what happens, or are you better at narrative than you let on?*

Leonard: There are certain times when I can get into narrative, that I can start a book with narrative and it works okay. Most of the time, though, I feel much more confident writing in scenes—in dramatic scenes—always, though, from a character's point of view, so that the scene takes the sound of the character. Then even the narrative—because you're looking through this character's eyes—has his sound. That's the way I've been doing it. Some people think that maybe I'm too much of a stickler for it, that I'm too rigid. But I would rather be a little too rigid than start to get sloppy with the points of view.

I get to know the main characters. I write about them in a notebook, where they begin as stock characters, and as I get to know them they come to life for me. I think I know where they fit in the book, and I put them to work. But I'm not that sure that a character is as important, say, as I think he's going to be, and another character will take over. Because the other character is a better talker, because he's more interesting, he takes over this role.

You say you put them to work. Marilyn Stasio, the crime critic for the New York Times Book Review, *says that she believes you don't see your characters so much as criminal or even evil, but as workers. In other words, you like writing about people who work according to some code or principle. Is that true?*

Leonard: No, it's not that way, but maybe that's the way it comes out. They're all working, they're all doing something.

Anthony Lukas has said that you're a wonderful and gentle person and yet you have a great sense of what he called "intuitive evil." How do you know so much about evil?

Leonard: Well, I don't know what intuitive evil is. My guys, for the most part, know when they are committing a crime. The nicer guys who have been into crime before, they take their chances. They know that if they get caught they're going to go to prison. That's the way it is. They are professional. I don't really know that much about what the other guys think if they get caught. They probably don't think they're going to get caught, because they're simple and they're dumb. I try and take the character as a person, first of all, rather than as the bad guy. I see them as human beings before I see them committing crimes. It's that simple. I see them offstage. I see them at odd times. I see them getting dressed, sneezing, eating breakfast. All that stuff. Little things. It's difficult for me to use the word evil.

Aside from the market research stuff, what do you think of the people who read your books. Who are they?

Leonard: They're everybody. A psychiatrist calls me to tell me that Chucky, who's a dope dealer in *Stick,* is suffering from a minimal brain dysfunction, that he is the authority on it. He wrote the paper on it, and I have him just right, and he wants to know where I got my information. I told him I made it up. Things like that. I hear from lawyers who claim they have met all of my characters. Then there's the letter from prison, from a guy in a federal penitentiary; he tells me what the guys are reading there, how I'm winning over more and more heroin sellers, but I haven't hit the crack and cocaine crowd yet, because they are younger and wilder, and less educated.

You once spent some time with Wilbert Rideau, the editor of the Angolite. *Did you get anything useful out of the visit?*

Leonard: Yes, I did. I didn't think it was going to be because I had this parade coming after me—a writer from *Newsweek,* a photographer, and a guy from the publishing company and two assistant wardens.

The first thing I said to him was, "What do you call the guards around here?" He said, "Oh, we call them 'sir.'" I thought I wasn't going to get anything from this guy. But I got what I wanted to know—the main thing.

Which was?

Leonard: Who decides what you watch on television, and actually he didn't have to answer it. I got the idea.

Do you read any prison newspapers?

Leonard: I read the *Angolite,* but I don't read it every month.

You've said that as a youngster one of the first and most important influences on you was films. Can you elaborate on that?

Leonard: The real influence I didn't discover until last year. I did a little piece for *Life* magazine. They asked me for a picture of myself, a very early picture, and then to write something about it, what it brought to mind. There's a favorite picture of mine, a snapshot that I had blown up of me standing in front of a car, actually on the side of the car with my mother and my sister, and I've got a little cap pistol in my hand, and my foot is on the running board. But I'm half turned, pointing the cap pistol at the camera. It's Bonnie Parker's pose, only her foot was on the front bumper. But the picture was taken in the summer of 1934, when I was about 9 years old, and it was within a month or so of Bonnie and Clyde being shot in northern Louisiana. That photograph of hers ran all over the country.

There were so many other pictures of people at the time—Machine Gun Kelly and Pretty Boy Floyd, and Ma Barker and her guys, all of these South-Midwest, where all these desperadoes were robbing banks in the '30s, when I was a little kid, reading the paper and doing a lot of train travel. We lived in New Orleans—I was born there. We lived in Dallas, in Oklahoma City, in Memphis, where all this was going on. I think that made a real impression on me.

In 1937, I was reading *All Quiet on the Western Front* in the *Detroit Times*. I didn't read the whole thing. I was just reading some episodes. I remember lying on the floor reading it, and then we put on a play in the school. I might have seen the movie first, but I don't remember. I'm sure it must have come out in '37 because I was in the fifth grade, and I wrote a little play and we had to put it on in the classroom. Couldn't put it on the stage because I needed the rows of desks for no-man's-land, for the barbed wire. The Americans on one side of the classroom, the Germans on the other, were shooting at each other. This was a Catholic school. The mother superior came in to see it, and she was the only audience we had.

You've never been particularly happy with what Hollywood has done with your own work. Why is that?

Leonard: If you buy my story, I say it can't be for the plot, and yet that's how they buy material in Hollywood. "Can you tell it in one or two sentences?" That's plot. You can't tell my stories like that. Plot is not that important, but my books have the appearance of film. They're in scenes, and they're loaded with dialogue, so the producers see it and say it's a movie. So many people, even out there, say, "My God, all you have to do is shoot the book. You know what you'd have?" I mean, they're exaggerating, but you still have to take out scenes and put in scenes and cut the dialogue way down.

So in other words they're not really interested in characters so much as they are with narrative? Do they get carried away with pyrotechnics?

Leonard: Yes, that's right. The adaptation becomes theatrical. That's what they do. You can see the actors acting, but you can't see my characters acting.

Do you have books that are currently slated for being films?

Leonard: Yeah, *Maximum Bob*. Donald Westlake is writing it for a four-hour miniseries for ABC. Ulu Grosbard is going to direct.

Who will get the lead?

Leonard: I don't know. I cast it in the book. I'd love to have Harry Dean Stanton. That might happen. But Ulu also likes Robert Duvall, and I do too.

I want to ask you about the crime-fiction business. It's a growing market, and you're one of the consistent best-sellers. Any idea, through fan mail or otherwise, why the market is growing?

Leonard: No. Ed McBain and I were on the "Today Show" about four years ago and we were asked that. We thought it was always successful—that's why we got in it. But we don't look at trends. I thought it was always very popular. Probably more than half of the books on the *Times'* list have something to do with crime.

Americans consistently say that they're worried about crime. Only recently, for instance, the House passed its new get-tough crime package. It's been surmised that there might be some correlation between the public's concern about crime and the growth of crime fiction. Do you think there's anything to it?

Leonard: No, I don't think there's any relationship at all, because there are different kinds of crime. Fictional crime is neat, with grown-ups getting into some kind of a crime where they either make it or they don't. But now it's all kids shooting each other, and it's all dope. A kid in the eighth grade pulls out a pistol and shoots somebody in the next row. That's not a movie. That's not a book.

Craig L. LaMay is director of media research at the Urban Institute at Northwestern University, Evanston, Illinois. He conducted this interview in 1992.

17

You Want Me to Read a What?

Peter A. Levin

There it was for all of us to see. And it wasn't a movie. It wasn't "L.A. Law." It was real. No Judge Wapner. No Perry Mason. A woman says she was raped. We hear her whole powerful testimony between her sobs.

Woman: "He had me on the ground, and I was trying to get out from underneath him because he was crushing me. And he had my arm and I was yelling, 'no,' and he slammed me back into the ground. And then he pushed my dress up and he raped me."

We see the defense attorney question her relentlessly:

Attorney: Did you have your panty hose on when you walked through the house?

Woman: I don't remember.

Attorney: Did you have your panty hose on when you walked across the lawn?

Woman: I don't remember.

Attorney: Did you have your panty hose on going down the stairs?

Woman: I don't remember.

And we see the defendant in compelling testimony fight to defend himself: "The issue here is I'm innocent. And how do you defend yourself from somebody who says the word 'rape' over and over again?"

For 10 days, the entire country was riveted by conflicting accounts of what happened during the predawn hours at the Kennedy estate in West Palm Beach, Florida, on Easter weekend 1991. With heavy doses of sex, money and celebrity, the trial had all the ingredients of good television drama.

155

And except for President Bush, audiences loved the show. Bush complained about televised trial coverage and the "filth and indecent material it carries into the nation's homes." But the trial proved to be a ratings bonanza for CNN, which offered live coverage of the proceedings. And the new cable channel Court TV got a major blast of publicity with its gavel-to-gavel coverage.

More importantly, the television coverage allowed people to see the American criminal justice system at work. They saw a hard-working judge who applied the law fairly to both sides. They saw defense lawyers and prosecutors committed to their cases. Viewers had the opportunity to learn about the admissibility of evidence, the rules of procedure, courtroom decorum, expert testimony, credibility of witnesses, burden of proof and reasonable doubt.

And hopefully viewers understood the need for many of the constitutional protections afforded defendants no matter what their family name. Few high school civics classes could have brought home these concepts more clearly.

But as I filed my reports from West Palm Beach each day, I realized that many significant civil cases were being tried in courtrooms throughout the country that were *not* being covered, much less televised. In a nation where most people get their news from television, the thought is sobering.

The problem, I've been told by many news directors, is that civil cases are boring and would not be of interest to viewers. But I don't believe that, mostly because I don't believe viewers' "interests" can be so narrowly defined. For example, the 1989 Joel Steinberg/Hedda Nussbaum trial for the murder of their illegally adopted daughter, Lisa, was high drama, but it really didn't affect most New Yorkers. And the trial of Zsa Zsa Gabor, who was able to turn an ordinary traffic arrest into comic opera, probably didn't affect the lives of most Californians.

While these criminal cases received heavy coverage, I would venture to say that important cases on employment discrimination, sexual harassment, product liability, surrogate parents, right to die, prayer in schools, abortion and prison overcrowding—civil cases all—were being ignored. I would also say that the media ignore them largely because they don't know *how* to cover them. Sometimes they don't even know how to *find* them. A criminal trial follows an arrest, but if you're going to cover civil court somebody has to know how to go to court and follow the docket. Civil cases also require some knowledge of the issues and the laws involved (read "training") or at the least a greater commitment of staff (read "resources"). By comparison, criminal cases are easy to follow; they're not usually that complex, and a reporter without any legal training can do an adequate job of covering them.

Civil cases, however, are where basic conflicts in our society are resolved. For every important case being argued before the U.S. Supreme Court, where cameras are not allowed, similar cases are being tried in courts of every state—and 45 states allow cameras of one kind or another in courtrooms. So often I'll see reports on television about rising auto insurance rates. And I wonder why the reporter didn't follow an actual fender-bender case in court to show one possible explanation. I'll see reports on how bankruptcies are rising and no stories on bankruptcy court showing *what* happens. I'll see stories on the harms of asbestos, with no stories about the special asbestos courts throughout the country created to handle the huge number of cases.

Former Vice President Quayle speaks about the litigation explosion caused by lawyers, generating controversy and a fair amount of news attention. But what about the substance of his claim? Cameras should go into courtrooms and show what's happening. Reporters could document how long a case took to get to trial and let the viewers make up their minds as to whether the suit was frivolous or whether it should have been settled without a trial.

It's upsetting to me as a lawyer and a reporter to know that many important sexual harassment cases were being heard in courtrooms before the Clarence Thomas/Anita Hill controversy. I couldn't interest news directors in covering these cases; and then, after the Senate hearings, there was a mad rush by stations to learn where these cases were being tried. I had two television networks contact me to help them find any kind of sexual harassment case.

I should add here that all my comments on the importance of covering civil cases are heavily influenced by the fact that as a practicing lawyer I handled primarily criminal cases, both as a prosecutor and public defender. My cases were heavily covered and high drama, but in the context of things they were just not that important—certainly not compared to many civil suits.

A few years ago I did a series of radio reports on an AIDS discrimination case that involved a partner at a national law firm who was fired for having AIDS. What made the case ironic is that the firm advertised heavily on television to get business. And its message was: "Trust us— we care about you." And yet the trial judge found that the firm certainly didn't care about this hard-working lawyer, who had received excellent performance reviews until contracting AIDS. The case was of major significance in that it was one of the first to look at AIDS in the workplace. It also raised a host of other legal issues affecting the workplace— such as employment contracts, other physical disabilities, pregnancy discrimination, sexual preference—but the case got no television coverage at all. One of the reasons was probably that the local TV stations were covering a far juicier AIDS case—a criminal case—involving a prisoner with AIDS who bit a guard. The case was rare, to say the least, and it probably affected none of the stations' viewers. But for the duration of the trial it ran in the top portion of every local newscast.

In July 1991, a three-year test of cameras in the federal courts began on an experimental basis in six federal district courts and two federal appeals courts. Although the coverage is presently limited to civil cases, at the end of the three years it could be expanded to criminal courts. And broadcast organizations are hopeful that all federal courts throughout the country, including the U.S. Supreme Court, will eventually be open to coverage.

But since the experiment has begun, the television stations in many of the chosen cities have done very little coverage. A perceived lack of interest in covering these civil cases could be a problem for broadcast groups whose long-term prospects in federal courts and the Supreme Court will be weighed against the results of the test.

As the media administrator for the federal court experiment in Philadelphia, I search for cases of interest for the local and regional stations to cover. I have encouraged our stations to cover nonsensational cases as proof of their interest in the judicial system. The cases are there to be found, and the stations are eager to cover them as long as they are prodded and told why a case is important. Since Pennsylvania is one of a handful of states that do not allow cameras in the courtroom except under extremely limited circumstances, the stations have been quite eager to cover these civil matters. The payoff, in terms of news of public affairs, has been enormous.

On the day the experiment began, for example, cameras covered the trial of *Edmonda Becker v. Unisys Corporation.* Although this age-discrimination case brought by a 62-year-old woman was hardly the usual stuff of news coverage, audiences loved it. And C-SPAN, CNN and Court TV were there to record the proceedings. I assisted the local public radio station in providing commentary during its live coverage, and each of the TV stations followed the case. The trial judge said that he later received more than 50 letters from people all over the country asking the outcome of the case (Unisys won).

More recently the stations covered a product-liability case filed by a 56-year-old stockbroker against the Lorillard Corporation. Peter Ierardi claimed he had developed mesothelioma, a rare form of cancer, from smoking Kent cigarettes, which in the 1950s had a micronite filter containing asbestos. What made this case unusual was that it was the first where a smoker sued a tobacco company for an illness unrelated to tobacco. Audiences followed the case closely, and some people who heard my reports even called me to register their thoughts on the verdict (Lorillard won). At the same time this case was being tried, there was a tobacco liability case waiting to be reargued before the U.S. Supreme Court.

One case that the stations had planned to cover was settled on the day the trial was to begin. Kim Certain, a track star at Villanova University who was training for the Olympics, charged that her coach had spread false rumors that she was having a lesbian affair with her high school coach. She sued Villanova for invasion of privacy and for libel and slander. The two big issues in the case that I had encouraged stations to examine were how women are treated in sports and whether there is discrimination against students based on sexual preference. I believe that the possibility of such critical coverage, and the adverse publicity it would create, figured prominently in the University's decision to settle.

In following civil cases in federal court, the local stations also found themselves covering many of Philadelphia's most politically newsworthy disputes. One concerned prison overcrowding. A federal judge had ordered the release of 175 inmates a week from city prisons, and the district attorney responded by filing a suit alleging that the judge's order was improper, that the city and the prisoners' attorneys had entered into an illegal contract to facilitate the prisoners' release. I suggested to the stations that they look at whether these monthly court battles over whether it's better to encourage lawlessness in neighborhoods by releasing prisoners or riots in the city jails are doing anything to improve Philadelphia. Reporters might want to step away from the hearings and explore why the city hasn't used alternatives to incarceration, such as boot camps, converted barges or mobile-home-type housing for prisoners. Reporters could also explore why it takes so long for inmates' cases to get to trial.

Another case involved Senator Arlen Specter's lawsuit against the U.S. Navy for its decision to close the Philadelphia Navy Shipyard. The Navy contended that the Base Closure Act specifically barred court intervention and that political leaders did not have the right to prevent the closure.

In the next few months there will be some other interesting civil cases the local television stations plan to follow: A female pathologist has sued Pennsylvania Hospital claiming that when she refused her boss's sexual advances he retaliated by having her perform autopsies of dead infants, knowing she was pregnant; a morning D.J. has filed suit against her former radio station for refusing to give her back her job after taking maternity leave; a Philadelphia Orchestra bassoonist had filed a breach of contract suit claiming the Orchestra failed to live up to an agreement guaranteeing him a more prestigious position; a hotel guest filed a lawsuit against Philadelphia's Hershey Hotel, claiming he was beaten by hotel employees and evicted from his room in the middle of the night because of a mixup over a previous unpaid bill; and a male employee is suing his employer claiming that as a highly religious and moral man, he was offended by fellow employees fondling their genital areas in his presence.

The point here, obviously, is that civil cases don't have to be boring. Many are as fascinating, some more so, as anything available in criminal court or on "L.A. Law." And if there are these many interesting cases in Philadelphia, I'm sure there have to be similarly compelling cases in other courts. For reporters unfamiliar with civil cases, there are some different issues to think about, and so I offer these suggestions:

1. Before the case starts, go to the attorneys on each side and get their positions. Once trial begins, they will be too busy to talk to you.

2. Make it a "people story" by talking to the parties involved. Criminal stories are about people in a rather obvious way; civil stories are about people, too, often in more subtle but equally provocative ways.

3. Read all the court papers that have been filed, not just the complaint. Criminal cases have a much shorter paper trail than civil cases do, and very few criminal cases have depositions—transcripts of sworn

question-and-answer sessions that the parties make prior to trial. Civil cases do, however; review them.

4. Get a list of all witnesses and interview them.

5. Get to know the legal context of the case by interviewing a law professor in your area.

6. Read any articles written about the issues involved in the case. A good place to begin is the guide to legal periodicals.

7. Talk to people in the court clerk's office as well as to the judge's law clerk or assistant.

8. Once the trial begins, do some reporting on the participants: What kind of judge is he or she? Who are the lawyers and what type of cases do they handle? Who are the jurors? How were they selected? Why?

9. And once the case is over, don't just report who won and who lost. Give reasons for the verdict. How will it affect similar cases? Does it set a precedent?

10. Look at the aftermath of the trial a number of months later. What are the parties doing? Have there been any changes made in the way they do business? Are there now similar suits being filed because of the verdict?

Without journalists covering these cases, average citizens have no idea what is taking place inside their courtrooms. Television news, particularly, has a critical role to play here, because television is where most citizens encounter the legal system. Very few Americans go to their local courthouse to watch a trial, and most have little contact with judges or lawyers, to say nothing of courtrooms. As television's eyes are permitted to peer ever further into our judicial system, it would be nice if they would open a little wider—and look around.

Peter A. Levin is a lawyer and reporter with "It's the Law" in Philadelphia.

18

Raskolnikov's Regret:
Covering Crime in Russia

Alexei Izyumov

The scene was not for the fainthearted—half a dozen naked bodies being readied for the postmortem examination at the Moscow criminal morgue. Yet the group of young police officers with white doctor's smocks thrown over their uniforms, pens and notebooks ready, tried to look enthusiastic: The class in the Moscow Police Academy was about to begin.

An hour later, when the medical part was over, only one of the visitors volunteered to stay on for the question-and-answer period. "How many bodies come every year? Who keeps the records? To whom are they reported?" he asked the chief of dissections. The answer was as he expected: "Even for you, the police, this information is classified. We'll give you some figures, but please, do not take notes and never tell the press."

That was 10 years ago, and the inquisitive visitor was me—a beginning investigative reporter trying to figure out one of the most closely held secrets of the Soviet society—its crime.

For generations Soviet people were told that crime just did not belong to the society of the proletariat. Whatever crime did occur was labeled another manifestation of the "birthmarks of capitalism." Much has changed since then. An anti-communist revolution started involuntarily by the man with the real birth mark devastated the old myths and unlocked the old secrets. Today to learn about crime a Russian does not have to put on a police uniform and count dead bodies in the morgue. Crime has become much more a public matter. It is true, of course, that the upheavals of perestroika led to the increase in the volume of crime itself. But thanks to glasnost, the increase in *reporting* about crime was far more dramatic. A form of reporting that was virtually nonexistent for 50 years now occupies the prize place in every major newspaper and on every TV channel.

For many Russians this explosion of crime information was a great shock. Some could not believe the situation was that bad, while others did not even want to know. Not infrequently during my travels and interviews in Russia, I heard people saying that the sudden flood of chilling reports on crime was making their life so miserable, and them so paranoid, that they would rather not hear about it.

Nowadays you will not meet many Russians who believe they can preserve their peace of mind by ignoring crime reports. With real crime increasing, such willful ignorance would be an impermissible luxury. At the same time, crime reporting has passed through the initial stage of "opening the closets" and is developing further, maturing and becoming more sophisticated and analytical. Borrowing both from the national traditions and the experience of the Western media, crime reporting is rapidly shaping up as a distinctive field of journalism in postcommunist Russia.

Over its century-long history, crime reporting in Russia has always been a combination of three distinctly different approaches: an analytical one, which emphasizes the socioeconomic as well as psychological roots of crime; the descriptive, which provides basic facts and figures about crime with little comment; and the sensational, which concentrates on the most notorious, "high-profile" crimes, often of a political nature. For brevity's sake I will call these approaches "Russian," "European" and "American," respectively.

The "Russian" style of crime reporting has much to do with the writings of Fyodor Dostoyevsky. Ever since *Crime and Punishment* men of letters in Russia were keen on studying the motives and circumstances that produce crime. With his penetrating analysis of the inner mind of the young criminal and powerful description of misery in mid-19th-century St. Petersburg, Dostoyevsky was one of the founders of the analytical tradition in the coverage of crime as a complex social phenomenon. Dostoyevsky's work influenced several generations of Russian journalists before the 1917 Bolshevik Revolution.

In contrast, the "European" style of crime reporting did not have any particular source of inspiration. Much like German, French or British newspapers of earlier periods, all big-city newspapers in 19th-century

Russia contained the "crime chronicle" section that reported all major crimes, police announcements and overall statistics of criminal offenses, arrests, indictments and so forth. Provincial newspapers did the same, including in their reports petty crime.

The "American" or sensationalist approach was not as wide-spread in prerevolutionary Russian media as were analytical and descriptive ones, yet the active political life of the late-19th and early 20th centuries provided not a few occasions for sensationalist writings. Suffice it to mention the coverage of the long series of terrorist assassinations, including those of Czar Aleksandr II in 1881 and Interior Minister Piotr Stolypin in 1911, or the famous Baylis affair—the sensational trial and acquittal of a Jew accused of the ceremonial killing of a boy in Kiev in 1911.

The Bolshevik Revolution of 1917 brought about radical changes in both the patterns of crime in Russia and its reporting. The destruction of the old authority, the ruthless persecution of opponents of the Communist regime, the hunt for the wealthy and the decimation of the church created an atmosphere of total lawlessness. The liberal press tried to report the Bolshevik crimes (such as the practice of mass hostage executions or Leon Trotsky's introduction of labor camps) but soon was silenced by the new rulers.

In the '20s, after the end of the civil war and during a period of relative liberalization and economic revival, the iron grip of "revolutionary justice" loosened somewhat. Reports on political persecution, which markedly subsided, were still under censorship, but news of common crime was reported in full.

Joseph Stalin's ascent to power in the 1930s changed the situation once again. Stalin reintroduced the concept of "revolutionary legality" on the most massive scale, subjecting the law completely to the interests of the ruling Communist elite. Millions were executed or went to the gulag archipelago as "enemies of the people." Under Stalin's rule, from 1929 to 1953, the press could not cover the true nature and extent of the purges, which, according to modern Soviet estimates, killed 50 million people. Instead, Stalin assigned the press the task of waging hate campaigns against the victims of his persecutions, the most famous of which were the 1937–38 "show trials" of his leading opponents.

Under Stalin the coverage of common crime also changed dramatically. The "father of the people" revived the old Marxist dogma of "withering away of crime," and in 1934, to make life fit with ideology, Stalin's censors banned the publication of any summary statistics on crime. Individual crimes could still be made public, but the old European tradition of full and meticulous reporting was severely curtailed. At the same time the analytical tradition was replaced with stories of hardened criminals turned model citizens through corrective labor and careful study of Communist textbooks. Sensationalism was reserved almost entirely for those charged with political crimes.

The Khrushchev era (1958-1964) saw a partial undoing of Stalin's legacy. The judicial system was largely depoliticized; millions of people were rehabilitated and allowed to return from prisons and labor camps. Khrushchev loosened press restrictions, allowing the emergence of such authors as Aleksandr Solzhenitsyn. Still, the press was on the short leash of the Communist Party apparatchiks, at whose command the media made criminals of Khrushchev's political opponents, such as the Nobel Prize-winning writer Boris Pasternak, and praised his government's highly irregular policies in judicial matters. In one famous case, two currency dealers in Moscow first convicted to prison terms were later condemned to death for the same crime when Khrushchev learned about their trial from the newspapers.

Like Stalin before him, and according to the same dogma, Khrushchev did not allow the publication of crime data, greatly hindering any resurgence of the European "facts only" approach to crime, and neither did he authorize the American style of sensationalist reporting. One exceptional case, however, was that of the "Mosgaz" serial killer, Moscow's counterpart to New York's notorious "Son of Sam." "Mosgaz" was the name of Moscow's gas company, and the killer would get into his victims' apartments by pretending to be a Mosgaz maintenance worker. As a kid I remember vividly the TV and radio announcers reporting the progress of the search and warning Moscovites not to open their doors to strangers. The publicity of the case ended abruptly, however, when the killer was caught.

Leonid Brezhnev, who ousted Khrushchev in 1964, preserved his predecessors' ideological attitude towards crime. Under his rule (1964-1982), censorship on crime coverage was so strict that even when publicity might have warned potential victims of their danger, the media were kept silent or uninformed. In the late '70s the country was shattered by a recurring series of murders—one year it was children, attacked by a maniac in elevators; another year it was women murdered in the streets of Moscow by a killer who only picked victims in red clothes. The most sinister case was the so-called "Vitebsk affair"—a series of 32 rape-murders committed over several years by a truck driver in Belorussia. None of these cases were reported in the press at the time, and people could only learn about the dangers that awaited them in the street through rumors or occasional briefings at the local police stations.

It was then that I started to inquire about the true extent of crime in the country. That interest led me to various people and institutions, but even my friends who were investigative police officers were not able to answer most of my questions. I remember a leading forensic expert and a professor at the police academy, after lecturing me about the incidence and history of serial murders, admitted he did not know the overall crime statistics even for the Moscow region.

Having no authorization for day-to-day crime reporting, Russian journalists writing on crime channeled their energy into the analysis of "isolated individual cases" that censors allowed them to cover. That, ironically, helped to reestablish the old Russian (analytical) tradition, almost extinct under Stalin. The *Literary Gazette,* the popular weekly of the writers union, became the main home of that tradition, setting forth a series of full-page accounts of crime-and-punishment stories. Other newspapers, such as *Komsomolskaya Pravda* and *Izvestia,* also contributed to that trend. The best investigative reporters of the period—Arkady Vaksberg, Olga Chaikovskaya, Evgeny Bogat, Yuri Schekochihin and others—are now known throughout the country.

Even the star reporters, though, were not permitted to tackle the potentially sensational cases, such as the 1969 assassination attempt on Brezhnev. The only "sensational" cases we were authorized to cover were those of "political criminals," such as the massive hate campaigns in the press against Aleksandr Solzhenitsyn and Andrei Sakharov in 1973, and several dissident and spy trials in the late '70s and early '80s.

Mikhail Gorbachev's rise to power in 1985 changed the rules of the game. From the very outset Gorbachev assigned the media the task of helping the Communist Party correct such social ills as crime, and while his idea of glasnost had little to do with genuine freedom of the press, it nonetheless gradually lifted the censorship on crime reporting and ended the era of old taboos.

It did so even as perestroika reforms greatly affected the crime situation in the country. In 1986 and '87, in the wake of a famous anti-alcohol campaign, crime markedly went down. But soon afterwards the prohibition laws led, as many predicted they would, to the emergence of a huge bootlegging industry. The prohibition laws were repealed, but the nation's crime situation quickly worsened, the result of economic difficulties, the decay of the law-enforcement system and the increase in ethnic clashes. New types of crime, such as large-scale drug dealing, racketeering and terrorism, came into being. Since 1991, with market reforms having brought ruinous inflation, unemployment and sharp disparities in income, crime has become a problem of catastrophic proportions.

Since 1989, general crime statistics for the whole country have at last been made public, and, as many expected, the crime rate in the Soviet Union is not lower but higher than in most Western countries, except for the United States.

More than that, in several crime-related categories—such as the absolute number of premeditated murders, the number of prison inmates and the number of executions—the Soviet Union turned out to be a world leader. In April 1990 *Pravda* reported that a record 21,500 murders were registered in the Soviet Union over the previous year, a figure which translates to an annual rate of 7.5 murders per 100,000 people. In most Western countries the respective figure is 1.1 to 1.6 murders per 100,000 population, which means that a Soviet citizen has a four- to five-times greater chance of dying a violent death than the average citizen in Japan, Britain or France. Since 1985 the number of murders in the USSR has been approximately equal to that of the United States, and this in a situation where the possession of firearms—an instrument of mortal crime widespread in the West—is strictly prohibited.

With the restoration of the old "European" tradition of crime reporting in the Russian media, most national, republican and provincial newspapers in the country have introduced crime departments to their pages and assigned journalists to that beat exclusively. The size of these departments and the incidence of their publication differ from newspaper to newspaper. Some, such as *Izvestia, Pravda* or *Nezavisimaya Gazeta* do it from time to time, while others, such as *Moskovskaya Pravda, Kuranty, Moskovskii Komsomoletz* or *Kommersant,* publish regular columns, usually once a week. Among Moscow newspapers the first full-fledged crime column has been introduced by the youth-oriented newspaper *Moskovskii Komsomoletz* (1992 circulation, 1.3 million). The column, appearing under the heading "chronicle of events," is written by a single reporter and gives a full account of crimes in the city, offers crime-safety advice, and sometimes includes pictures of lost persons and wanted criminals.

All-national ("central") newspapers publish summary crime figures once or twice a year but run partial summaries and individual crime stories much more frequently. With the growth of crime, crime-safety departments have become a regular feature of the major newspapers, such as *Izvestia* (1992 circulation, 2.8 million) and *Argumenty i Fakty* (2.6 million).

Because of stricter censorship, Soviet television has lagged behind the print media somewhat, but since 1988 it too has introduced regular programs on crime. Now four major channels operating from Moscow and St. Petersburg have their daily or weekly crime reports. Channel 1, which until very recently was an all-union channel but now belongs to the Russian Republic's "Ostankino" company, runs the weekly "Internal Ministry Report," covering crime all over the country. Russian TV (Channel 2) has a daily special called "Criminal Channel," and Moscow-City TV (Channel 3) offers daily briefings on the crime situation by the city police. St. Petersburg TV (Channel 5) covers crime in its "600 Seconds" evening news program. In sharp contrast with the pre-perestroika "no-crime-exists-in-the-USSR" attitude, these programs show millions of viewers real-life pursuits and arrests and chilling scenes of crimes—in full color and at close range.

This new flood of previously banned "raw" information about crime has somehow overshadowed the classical analytical tradition in crime reporting. The long investigative stories of the type *Literaturnaya Gazeta* was famous for in the '70s are no longer popular, and today the analytical style concentrates on issues rather than individual stories. Among the topics most frequently discussed are the crisis of the law-enforcement system, the poor state of prisons, the abolition of the death penalty and the impact of economic reforms on the incidence of crime. To examine these problems the newspapers usually employ a variety of techniques, including in-depth interviews with experts, roundtable discussions, public opinion surveys and statistical comparisons with other countries.

In the last months of 1991, for example, Russian newspapers published volumes of analytical material on the state of the prison system. The extensive coverage was prompted by the unprecedented strike of inmates in November, in which 80 percent of the Russian prisons and labor camps took part. The strikers were protesting their miserable conditions, the cruelty of guards and the harshness of their sentences, and they drew support from human-rights activists and got sympathetic coverage in the press. *Izvestia* and *Literaturnaya Gazeta* both noted the abnormally high size of the prison population (780,000 prisoners and 200,000 held for investigation). *Moscow News* stressed the irrelevance of most of the "economic-crime" laws in an era of market reforms; *Kommersant* drew unfavorable comparisons with other countries; and *Argumenty i Fakty* turned its attention to the lives of inmates after their release from prison. The massive calls for reforms helped to speed up the long-awaited revision of the Russian Criminal Code in December 1991.

Perhaps most interesting in the new age of Russian crime reporting is the way in which glasnost freedoms and rapidly increasing media competition have given a powerful boost to sensationalism. Breathtaking disclosures of corruption, terrorist plots and the grandiose machinations of the rich and famous are flooding the nation's newspapers and TV screens as never before. Crimes or alleged crimes involving major political figures are leading the way. Prior to the August 1991 coup attempt, the major stories of this type were the so-called "Uzbek affair" and the "ANT" affair.

The first case, widely reported by all the major newspapers, dealt with an extensive corruption network that involved scores of high Communist Party officials in the Central Asian republic of Uzbekistan and in the central government in Moscow. The unusual publicity of the investigation led some of Gorbachev's colleagues to retire and ensured hero status and parliament seats for the two principal investigators. The second case, often called "ANT-gate," resulted from the effort of a major defense-related corporation to sell a dozen tanks to a foreign customer without the proper authorization. Again, scores of high officials, including then-Prime Minister Nickolai Ryzhkov, came under such extensive press criticism that several were forced to quit their posts.

In the aftermath of the August revolution it would almost seem as though some things are much the same. Political cases are still most likely to become major media sensations—common crimes rarely do— though this is quite natural in the highly politicized atmosphere of today's Russian life. The upcoming trial of the junta members and an investigation into alleged secret Communist Party accounts in foreign banks have generated enormous press interest, as has the role of the former leaders of the USSR, including Gorbachev himself, in the bloody military interventions in the Baltics in January 1991.

At the same time there have been exceptions. The fatal shooting in St. Petersburg of the popular rock singer Igor Talkov has received extensive coverage, as have the "Artyom Tarasov affair" and the "Sheremetievo dollars" case. Tarasov, the pioneering Russian millionaire, is alleged to have appropriated several million dollars from his company account in Paris and is now on the run somewhere in Europe. The second story deals with the ongoing investigation of the 1989 theft at Moscow's international airport of part of $3 million in bank notes from the Republican National Bank of New York.

At the moment, however, overall coverage of sensational crimes in Russian media is still fairly modest by Western standards. With stronger competition and the advent of the advertising age this category of reporting will increase. The high public demand for sensational fare has already brought into being several specialized publications, such as *Sovershenno Secretno* (Top Secret) and *Criminal Cronicle*. The TV version of "Top Secret" was recently introduced on the Russian channel.

Taken as a whole, the new age of crime reporting in Russia is a welcome change in a country living through turbulent times. It helps to dispel the dreams of Marx and Lenin that the Communist experiment would wither away crime, and as well it permits the media to pay back the moral debt they incurred during the long years of censorship. There are many unpleasant truths the former Soviet peoples must face, and the incidence and nature of crime are among them. Showing these things begins the task of coping with the realities of a new Russia.

Alexei Izyumov is a columnist for Newsweek, *a fellow at The Freedom Forum Media Studies Center, and visiting professor of economics at the University of Louisville.*

IV
Review Essay

19

Glimpses of Gotham

Robert W. Snyder

New York by Gas-Light and Other Urban Sketches
George G. Foster (N. Orr, 1850;
republished by University of California Press, 1990)

How the Other Half Lives: Studies among the Tenements of New York
Jacob Riis (Charles Scribner's Sons, 1890;
republished by Dover, 1971)

The Autobiography of Lincoln Steffens
Lincoln Steffens (Harcourt, Brace and Company, 1931)

Weegee by Weegee: An Autobiography
Arthur Fellig (Ziff-Davis Publishing Co., 1961)

Crime Scene
Mitch Gelman (Times Books, 1992)

At the heart of crime reporting lies a massive irony: Although crime news usually means fast-breaking daily stories, the practices, purposes and postures of American crime reporters have remained largely unchanged for more than 150 years. With all the changes in news organizations and technology, their craft remains the same. They titillate with sex and violence, astound with explorations of the inner city, and warn of what to fear on a walk down a dark side street. Then they depart—leaving readers thrilled, frightened, confused, and scarcely more knowledgeable about why crimes exist and what they can do about them.

The very characteristics that make the crime story compelling—immediacy and drama—give it a short shelf life. Structured around what basic facts can be unearthed under a pressing deadline, crime news contains little of the analysis or contextual information that helps put events in perspective. War correspondents reporting daily carnage can expect to see their dispatches surrounded by stories explaining how the battle fits into a grand strategy. But crime reporters usually see their stories run next to other breaking crime stories. Together they set their own awful context: murder and mayhem, over and over again, for no explainable reason.

If the problems of crime reporting in American newspapers are clear, how and why they exist, and what to do about them, are harder to determine. The logical people to ask are the reporters themselves. But crime reporters are a notoriously unreflective bunch. And the best of them usually see their days on the beat as a prelude to a more distinguished career. For most journalists, crime reporting is something to be left behind, like adolescent high jinks: a phase to be recalled in moments of nostalgia, but worthy of little more.

One of the few places where crime reporting is explored and put in context is in the books of reporters who covered the mayhem, either in their apprentice days or as the mainstay of their careers. Their words explicate the relationship between crime and big-city newspapers—and they have a much longer shelf life than the authors' daily articles. Read in sequence, they illuminate the history of crime and its journalism, providing a sense of change over time to the seemingly unchanging story of crime news.

Under closer examination, crime news turns out to be concerned with far more than episodes of lawbreaking. Since the creation of modern metropolitan dailies, crime reporting has been a chronicle of life in inner cities. As such, it has defined America's ethnic and racial minorities, from the immigrant Irish of the 19th century to the African-Americans of the 20th. And it has often defined them through stereotypes, or at the very least through disaster stories and little else. The result has been a skewed and pathological picture.

Crime reporting has been done largely—although not exclusively—by men. Yet it is profoundly concerned with men and women—and sex. In the 19th century, when most Americans saw women as the caretakers of morality, crime reporters spilled much ink over prostitution. In the

20th, when women are less likely to be seen as guardians of social purity, crime reporting involving women has become more blatantly sensational—and less avowedly moralistic.

We know a time, an era and a place by the crimes that fascinate it. The discourse about crime that reporters simultaneously shape and respond to is partly an attempt to define morality, shared public concerns, and the nature of city life. And of all American cities, the city whose crime reporting is most worth examining is New York.

Daily newspapers as we know them—cheap, mass-produced and mass-marketed—first appeared in New York in the 1830s. The City's size, economic power and human diversity made it a dynamic source of news. It is no accident that the 1836 murder of prostitute Ellen Jewett, the coverage of which marks a critical point in the evolution of the reporter as an investigator—was reported out of New York City. And as one of the premier cities of American journalism, New York became a capstone in many reporters' careers—and thus a place to reflect on in print.

Mass-circulation newspapers—and crime reporting—grew hand in hand with the city. In 1800 New York had a population of 60,000. By 1850, immigration, trade and industrialization had transformed New York into a metropolis of more than half a million. Day by day the City grew bigger, more complicated, and harder to know firsthand. Older inhabitants, who remembered the more homogeneously Anglo-American city of the late-18th and early 19th century, lamented the disappearance of a common idea of order and morality.

In this confusion, the metropolitan reporter and the mass circulation "penny press" became the guides for a readership confounded by the city's diversity—and alternately fascinated and repelled by the crime, vice and poverty at its core. The city and the metropolitan newspaper grew hand in hand. Reporters staked out the courts as the one place where the poor, the criminals and the immigrants of the city regularly appeared. In their stories they captured the cruelties, inequalities and exoticism that seemed to be ever more at the core of the city. And so was born the enduring role of the crime reporter as a guide to the mysteries of inner-city life.

Into this whirlwind stepped George Foster, a roving reporter, editor and poet who arrived in New York City in 1842. As one of the first generation of journalists to write for mass-circulation daily newspapers, he broke with the old practice of writing up dull descriptions of official meetings and events and plunged into the back alleys of the City. As an on-and-off reporter for Horace Greeley's *Tribune,* there was no subject that enthralled him more than crime.

In a city where so many people were strangers to one another, Foster was fascinated by fraud, deception and misleading appearances. As a native-born American, he was suspicious of all who differed from a Protestant, Anglo-Saxon norm. As a product of that middle-class culture of restraint, sobriety and virtuous women that we now call Victorianism, he believed that the bedrock of society was a home presided over by a dutifully pure female.

As such, Foster was alternately fascinated and repelled by prostitution. More than a century after he collected his newspaper sketches into *New York by Gaslight,* this is the topic where his writing sparkles. Foster reveled in the "festivities of Prostitution, the orgies of pauperism, the haunts of theft and murder, the scenes of drunken and beastly debauch" that distinguished life in New York. Women soliciting on the streets, women in brothels, women in dance halls, women in lewd stage shows, women conning sailors in drunken dance halls—Foster found them all compelling, and he covered them with a mixture of sympathy, lechery and high-minded moralizing. His purpose, he wrote, was to "lay bare the fearful mysteries of darkness in the metropolis,...to discover the real facts of the actual condition of the wicked and wretched classes—so that Philanthropy and Justice may plant their blows aright."

Perhaps. But equally plausible is Foster's desire to take his readers for a swim in the swamps of vice under the pretext of exploring pressing social issues. Foster claimed to be confronting problems to solve them. A skeptic might say he was exploiting them. As a journalist, Foster's greatest bequest is his willingness to go hunting for news in the farthest corners of the city. His worst is his tendency to cloak his voyeurism in a self-righteous search for truth. As Thomas Leonard has observed of sensationalizing reporters and reformers, "It has never been easy to draw a line between the committed and the crass."

Foster died in 1856 of a fever caught covering a fire in Philadelphia. But the role of the police reporter as illuminator of the inner city outlived him. And no one did more with the role—or reveal more of its limitations—than Jacob Riis.

An immigrant from Denmark, Riis reported on a New York that was different from Foster's. Ever-increasing numbers of Italian and

Jewish immigrants were adding a new layer of diversity to the City. In terms of murder rate—always the best-documented barometer of crime—the City was much safer than the more violent one of the mid-19th century. Yet the arrival of new immigrants, coupled with economic difficulties, created widespread unease about order in the city—and more than a hint of anti-immigrant sentiment. Although Riis lived in a New York that was less violent than Foster's, he was profoundly concerned about what would happen if New York came to breed an impoverished inner-city criminal class.

Riis is best remembered for his exposés of immigrant poverty and his advocacy of housing reform. But as a journalist, he was above all a police reporter. He explored the slums while tagging along on police raids. His depictions of immigrant life were strongly flavored by his fear that these newcomers posed a distinct threat to public order—a fear partly attributable to the fact that he encountered the immigrants at crime scenes. Above all, he never really rose above the most base stereotypes and prejudices of his age.

Riis' *How the Other Half Lives* is a classic of urban journalism. And like most classics, as Mark Twain observed, people praise it without reading it. Its photographs are powerful, although when first published they had to be redrawn because the half-tone reproduction process had not yet been perfected. Yet some of Riis' shots are clearly staged, and many of them are set up to show his subjects at their most degraded—a fine way to substantiate his contention that tenements were a breeding ground of immorality and revolution, but a poor recognition of the immigrants' intelligence and ingenuity.

When he asked why crime and poverty existed in the slums, Riis came up with two answers: bad housing conditions and immigrant immorality, which was partly the product of their environment. The emphasis on housing could at times be simplistic, but Riis did worse when he participated in his age's penchant for ethnic and racial stereotyping. Although an ostensibly "independent" reporter, he did little more than parrot stock assessments of inhabitants of the ghetto. "The Italian," he wrote, "is gay, light-hearted and if his fur is not stroked the wrong way, inoffensive as a child." On the Jews: "Money is their God. Life itself is of little value compared with even the leanest bank account."

Reporters pride themselves on their ability to enter into the most closed of environments, and at times this gives them an incentive to exaggerate the impenetrability of the neighborhoods they cover. Riis certainly did that in Chinatown, which he dismissed as an alien conspiracy in the heart of New York. True to his craft's emphasis on what can be made to appear bizarre and titillating, he waxed eloquent on opium and white slavery in Chinatown; true to his age's racism against the Chinese, which had just led to strong federal limits on Chinese immigration, he portrayed Chinatown's residents as a threatening force. "He is by nature as clean as the cat," he wrote of the Chinese immigrant, "which he resembles in his traits of cruel cunning and savage fury when aroused."

If Riis' pronouncements are startling in an age when Chinese-Americans are considered a "model minority," they are a reminder of how the basest of prejudices go unexamined in their own time, and how the bravest of reporters can blindly follow the social and intellectual currents of their day. They are also a reminder of the version of immigrant life that appears when police reporters venture into neighborhoods with the primary motive of uncovering newsworthy crimes, cruelties and confusion.

In retrospect, *How the Other Half Lives* expresses the less generous sentiments of its time. More representative of the expansive spirit of urban reform in the late-19th and early 20th century, known now as the Progressive Era, is Lincoln Steffens' *Autobiography*. If Riis was limited by his tendency to see things from the perspective of a police raid, his contemporary Steffens produced crime reporting with a refreshing difference: a tendency to report crime from the victim's point of view. It is this empathy that makes Steffens' *Autobiography* delightful and instructive more than 50 years after its publication.

Steffens arrived on the police beat with a university education that left him with a taste for moral questions and a stint covering Wall Street that attuned him to the significance of power and political economy. He quickly grasped that the police beat was a way to get a practical education in the workings of the City. "The police," he wrote, "meant to me a dark, mysterious layer of the life of a great city into which I had not yet penetrated."

Making the rounds of disasters, observing the making of scandals, Steffens acquired a solid sense of the politics of news and how relations between reporters and sources and institutions shape what gets into the paper. His chapter "I Make a Crime Wave," in which he recounts how he and Riis created a panic by aggressively going after new stories, remains a masterpiece of how journalistic practice defines public agendas. For all the fear they inspired, it wasn't that more crimes were being committed—only that more of them were getting into the paper.

At the scenes of shrieks and fires and accidents, Steffens encountered the immigrants of the Lower East Side, among them the Jews. Instead of recoiling in fear or hostility, he set out to see life in New York from their point of view, going so far as to become a fan of the Yiddish theater and a regular attender of synagogue services.

Steffens gained an appreciation of immigrant life from the inside out, and went beyond the facts of the stories to their deeper human qualities. He wrote clear and wrenching reports on the smallest details of immigrants' lives, from the pain of generational conflict between pious immigrant Jews and their assimilated children to the pathetic conflict between a harassed prostitute and a mother who wants to shield her children from the sight of the prostitute's assignations.

Steffens came to see the immigrant Jews as more than a source of colorful copy. To him, they were a source of wisdom, with a unique integrity and significance. When he became editor of the *Commercial Advertiser,* he brought onto his staff Abraham Cahan, the immigrant Jewish socialist journalist who would later earn fame as editor of *Forward.* "I had enjoyed and profited by my police reporter's interest in the picturesque Ghetto, and I knew it was good—good journalism and good business—for my reporters to follow and report the happenings over there. It increased our circulation; the Jews read the *Commercial,* and it broadened the minds of the staff and our reader." It also showed where police reporting could lead if it was done with curiosity and a strong conscience.

In retrospect, Steffens' turn-of-the-century introduction to the police beat and to New York took place before crime had acquired many of its defining characteristics in the 20th century. The late-19th century actually saw a decline in murder in New York, to be followed by an increase into the early 1930s, then another decline and a terrible rise in the early '60s that has not yet significantly abated. Prohibition, and the consequent creation of nationwide organized crime, was still ahead. So were the great black and Latino migrations to the City that would make crime one more element in the complex web of racial and ethnic relations. New York in the 1890s was also, at least in Steffens' view, a "moral community with a conscience." Even allowing for exaggerations, there was at least some element of truth to his statement: it was that conscience to which Steffens, reformers and radicals appealed, and they were not always rebuffed.

But as the 20th century progressed, the gaps and contradictions in that conscience grew ever more pronounced. The rise of a consumer culture rooted in self-gratification, the cynicism of Prohibition, the coarsening effect of the poverty and the cancer of racism all eroded what moral consensus Steffens had been able to discern. When he published his *Autobiography* in 1931, he was already referring to it in the past tense. And with good reason. New York was then experiencing the highest murder rates in living memory; it was a national center for organized crime; and its social fabric strained under the weight of the Depression.

The veneer of moral judgment that gilded crime news in George Foster's time was falling apart. Although moralistic crime coverage did not cease to exist in the mid-20th century, it grew to share news space with a more raw, less moralistic approach that found its greatest expression in the photography of Arthur Fellig, better known as Weegee. Where earlier journalists took care to distinguish between the pure and the profane, in his autobiography *Weegee by Weegee* the photographer explicitly blurred them. "This was the East Side of the 1920s, with its Grand Street Playhouse, Henry Street settlement house, Educational Alliance, music schools, synagogues and whorehouses," he wrote of the Manhattan neighborhood where he grew up. "I like them and attended them all."

"I have no inhibition, and neither has my camera," he wrote. "What may be abnormal to you is normal to me." An Austrian immigrant and the son of a peddler who became a rabbi, Weegee was a free-lance photographer who worked out of the police headquarters in lower Manhattan. "Crime was my oyster, and I liked it...my post-graduate course in life and photography," he wrote.

Making the nighttime round of murder scenes with his camera, Weegee was firmly grounded in the tradition of the New York crime reporter, guiding his audience through the maze of the City: Fourth Avenue between 13th and 14th streets was great for pickups; the police station on East 51st Street was a hot spot for crimes committed in the neighborhoods of the rich and famous. Yet where previous guides had alluded to what went on beyond closed doors, or described it in censorious tones, Weegee described himself as an enthusiastic participant in the City's sexual underground. What was once private was now to be made fully public.

Like Riis and Steffens before him, Weegee's beat took him to the tragedies of the City's poor, which he recorded in photos like his wrenching shot of two women tormented by grief at a tenement fire. But he also received great recognition for his photographs of mob killings. Weegee grasped that in a big city the only way a gangster could make a big reputation was by getting plenty of press. "No racketeer on the FBI's list of the top 10 public enemies made the grade until he had been photographed by Weegee," he bragged. "I was finally honored for my contributions by being called (by the boys) the official photographer for Murder, Inc." No rubout was complete, he said, until he had photographed the victim.

In his photographs of gangland killings, Weegee believed that he had "photographed the soul of the City I knew and loved." It was a complicated and contradictory soul, much more so than the one Foster had tried to fathom. In photographs like "Their first murder," which shows people at a crime scene expressing emotions that include joy, curiosity, pain and discomfort, Weegee captured a city which could by no stretch of the imagination be called a "moral community."

What kind of community it *would be* in any meaningful sense grew murkier as the 20th century drew to a close. The years after World War II saw a massive population exchange in New York, as the older European immigrants and their children moved to the suburbs, to be replaced by black Americans moving up from the South and Puerto Ricans. Instead of a golden door, too many of the newcomers found poverty and hostility—and an increasingly murderous urban environment. The climbing crime rates of the 1960s heralded a new crime wave, greater than any in the City's past, which fostered the murderous years of the late 1980s, when New York drew ever closer to the 2,000 murders-per-year mark. Into this mayhem walked Mitch Gelman, a rookie police reporter for *New York Newsday*. *Crime Scene,* the story of his initiation into the police beat in New York City, shows how little—and how much—has changed since Foster, Riis and Steffens worked the beat.

As in almost all reminiscences of entries into journalism, Gelman tells a story of ambition, lost innocence and idealism tested in adversity. And, like his predecessors, Gelman makes sure to establish himself as an accredited guide to the back streets of the City. What sets Gelman's story apart—and here it is reminiscent of Steffens—is his attention to how he practices his craft as a reporter, and whom he practices it with. Gone is the all-male camaraderie of the police shack. Two of his colleagues are Latinos. Gone also are the days when cops and reporters could be assumed to be from the same working-class ethnic background. Part of Gelman's task is not only to cross the blue line that separates cops from the rest of the world, but to move as an upper-middle-class liberal Jew in a world of working-class Catholic ethnics. In Foster's time the Irish were the terrors of the City's slums. In Gelman's, they are at the core of the police force.

It is a police force that manages information with a well-developed sense of hierarchy, secrecy and public relations. Next to Gelman's wranglings, Steffens' access to the NYPD looks absolutely open. Part of the problem is a changed political sensibility: Gelman, clearly influenced by the aura of the '60s, is skeptical of authority. The problem also occurs, one suspects, because reporters of Gelman's generation rarely see the police beat as a lifelong job. Unlike some of their older predecessors who saw it as a life's calling, reporters of Gelman's generation see it as a stepping-stone. And journalists who hope to move off the beat in a few years are not likely to develop the shared perspectives and friendships that make for a cozy and sometimes corrupt relationship between a reporter and a police department.

Like most police reporters, Gelman emphasizes violent crime—which actually absorbs very little of a policeman's day. The reality of tedious patrols and impromptu social work that form so much of a police officer's day find no place in this book. But what does appear is a highly developed sense of how race and crime have become deeply intertwined issues in New York, if not in urban America generally. Gelman is acutely aware that blacks and Latinos are disproportionately victims of the City's violent crime, and his outrage at their victimization is a healthy change from the old days when the only newsworthy crime victims were white. The change is partly the result of black demands to be taken seriously as citizens, and partly the work of a reporter who recognizes suffering and injustice when he sees them.

What Gelman's book means for the future of reporting on crime is hard to say. As a print journalist covering hard news on the police beat, he is something of an anachronism. More and more Americans are getting their news from television, and more and more television shows present "reenactments" of crimes that blur the relationship between entertainment and journalism. Perhaps newspapers will become the last refuge of journalists who want to do real reporting on crime. If they do, journalists can learn something from the history of their craft: the need

to transcend widely held stereotypes of the moment, the value of looking at crime from the victim's point of view and the dangers of letting
crime reporting become the only kind of reporting done on the people
who live in inner cities.

By understanding where they have come from, journalists can better
grasp where they are going. And in the writings of past generations of
crime reporters, they may catch a reflection of the deep-rooted flaws—
and strengths—of their own work.

Robert W. Snyder, a historian and author, is managing editor of the Media
Studies Journal.

For Further Reading

American Bar Association. *Advisory Committee Reardon Report of the ABA Advisory Committee on Fair Trial and Free Press.* Chicago: ABA, 1964.

_____. *ABA Standards for Criminal Justice.* Vol. 2. Boston: Little Brown, 1980. See Chapter 8, "Fair Trial and Free Press," and "Commentary," pp. 7–14, 52–57, 60–61.

_____. *The Rights of Fair Trial and Free Press: The American Bar Association Standards.* Chicago: ABA, 1981.

The American University Law Review. "Symposium Issue on the Selection and Function of the Modern Jury." Washington, D.C.: American University. Vol. 40, Winter 1991.

Best, Joel. *Threatened Children: Rhetoric and Concern About Child victims.* Chicago: University of Chicago Press, 1990.

Breslin, Jimmy. *The World According to Breslin.* New York: Ticknor and Fields, 1984.

Buchanan, Edna. *Never Let Them See You Cry.* New York: Random House, 1992.

Burger, Warren E. "Interdependence of Judicial and Journalistic Independence." *New York State Bar Journal,* 47:453, October 1975.

Bush, Chilton. *Free Press and Fair Trial: Some Dimensions of the Problem.* Athens: University of Georgia Press, 1971.

Capote, Truman. *In Cold Blood.* New York: Signet, 1965.

Carlson, James M. *Prime-Time Law Enforcement: Crime Show Viewing and Attitudes Toward the Criminal Justice System.* New York: Praeger, 1985.

Cohen, Jeremy. "Cameras in the Courtroom and Due Process: A Proposal for a Qualitative Difference Test." *Washington Law Review,* 47:277, 1982.

Crane, Stephen. "Bowery Tales." *An Omnibus.* New York: Alfred A. Knopf, 1952.

Dreschel, Robert E. *News Making in the Trial Courts.* New York: Longman, 1983.

Fellig, Arthur. *Weegee by Weegee: An Autobiography.* New York: Ziff-Davis, 1961.

Foster, George G. *New York by Gas-Light and Other Urban Sketches.* Berkeley: University of California Press, 1990.

Frank, Jerome. *Courts on Trial—Myth and Reality in American Justice.* Princeton, N.J.: Princeton University Press, 1949.

Freedman, Warren. *Press and Media Access to the Criminal Courtroom.* Westport, Conn.: Greenwood Press, 1988.

Friendly, Alfred, and Ronald L. Goldfarb. *Crime and Publicity: The Impact of News on the Administration of Justice.* New York: The Twentieth Century Fund, 1967.

Gelman, Mitch. *Crime Scene.* New York: Times Books, 1992.

Gerald, J. Edward. *News of Crime: Courts and Press in Conflict.* Westport, Conn.: Greenwood Press, 1983.

Gerbner, George. *Violence and Television Drama: A Study of Trends and Symbolic Functions.* Philadelphia: University of Pennsylvania Press, 1970.

Gordon, Margaret, and Stephanie Riger. *The Female Fear.* New York: The Free Press, 1989.

Graber, Doris. *Crime News and the Public.* Westport, Conn.: Greenwood Press, 1980.

Iyengar, Shanto. *Is Anyone Responsible? How Television Frames Political Issues.* Chicago: University of Chicago Press, 1991. See Chapter 4, "Effects of Framing on Attributions of Responsibility for Crime and Terrorism."

Jencks, Christopher. "Is Violent Crime Increasing?" *The American Prospect,* Winter 1991.

Kane, Peter E. *Murder, Courts and the Press: Issues in Free Press/Fair Trial.* Carbondale, Ill.: Southern Illinois University Press, 1986.

Malcolm, Janet. "The Journalist and the Murderer." *The New Yorker,* March 13 and 20, 1989.

McGinniss, Joe. *Fatal Vision.* New York: Signet, 1989. The epilogue to the 1989 edition is McGinniss' response to the March 1989 *New Yorker* article "The Journalist and the Murderer" by Janet Malcolm, and contains several insights to the journalistic approach to violent crime.

Minow, Newton N., and Fred H. Cate. "Who is an Impartial Juror in an Age of Mass Media?" *The American University Law Review* 40:631, Winter 1991.

National Center for State Courts. *Managing Notorious Cases.* Williamsburg, Va.: National Center for State Courts, 1992.

President's Commission on the Assassination of President John F. Kennedy. *Report of the President's Commission on the Assassination of President John F. Kennedy.* Warren Commission, 1968.

Reardon, Paul C., and Daniel Clifton. *Fair Trial and Free Press.* Washington, D.C.: American Enterprise Institute for Public Policy Research, 1968.

Riis, Jacob A. *How the Other Half Lives: Studies among the Tenements of New York.* Cambridge, Mass.: Belknap Press of Harvard University Press, 1970.

Runyon, Damon. *Trials and Other Tribulations.* Philadelphia: J.B. Lippincott, 1947.

Schiller, Dan. *Objectivity and the News: The Public and the Rise of Commercial Journalism.* Philadelphia: University of Pennsylvania Press, 1981. Schiller's book includes a substantial and critical examination of the early *Police Gazette,* and the magazine's role in defining the "newsworthy."

Shaw, David. Pulitzer Prize-winning series on the *Los Angeles Times'* coverage of the McMartin preschool case. *Los Angeles Times,* Jan. 19–22, 1990.

Shaw, Donald, and Maxwell McCombs. *The Emergence of American Political Issues: The Agenda-Setting Function of the Press.* St. Paul, Minn.: West, 1977.

Simon, David. *Homicide: A Year on the Killing Streets.* New York: Houghton Mifflin, 1991.

Simons, Howard, and Joseph Califano. *The Media and the Law.* New York: Praeger, 1976.

Sindall, Robin. *Street Violence in the Nineteenth Century: Media Panic or Real Danger?* New York: Columbia University Press, 1990.

Steffens, Lincoln. "I Make a Crime Wave." *The Autobiography of Lincoln Steffens.* New York: Harcourt, Brace and Co., 1931.

Stevens, John. *Sensationalism and the New York Press.* New York: Columbia University Press, 1991.

Surette, Ray. *The Media and Criminal Justice Policy: Recent Research and Social Effects.* Springfield, Ill.: Thomas, 1990.

Warr, Mark. "America's Perceptions of Crime and Punishment." Chapter 1 in Joseph F. Sheley's *Criminology.* Belmont, Calif.: Wadsworth, 1991. Warr's chapter is a noted criminologist's concise summary of the media's treatment of crime, including discussions of "newsworthiness," distortion in print and broadcast and distortion's effects.

Warshow, Robert. "The Gangster as Tragic Hero." *The Immediate Experience: Movies, Comics, Theatre and Other Aspects of Popular Culture.* Garden City, N.Y.: Doubleday & Co., 1964.

Weegee. *Naked City.* New York: Essential Books, 1945.

Wicker, Tom. *A Time to Die.* New York: Times Books, 1975.

Index